STIG NYBO

WITH LIZ ALEXANDER, PHD.

AWAKENING THE SUPER SAVER
IN PURSUIT OF RETIREMENT READINESS

TRANSFORM TOMORROW

WILEY

John Wiley & Sons, Inc.

Library of Congress Cataloging-in-Publication Data:

Nybo, Stig.
   Transform tomorrow : awakening the super saver in pursuit of retirement readiness/ Stig Nybo with Liz Alexander, Ph.D.
        pages cm
   Includes bibliographical references and index.
   ISBN 978-1-118-53736-7 (hbk. : alk. paper) ; ISBN 978-1-118- 57463-8 (ebk); ISBN 978-1-118-57282-5 (ebk); ISBN 978-1-118-57274-0 (ebk)
   1. Retirement—United States. 2. Retirement income—United States—Planning. I. Alexander, Liz.   II. Title.
      HQ1063.2.U6N93 2013
      306.3'80973—dc23

                                                            2012041907

Printed in the United States of America.

10 9 8 7 6 5 4 3 2 1

This book is dedicated to my father, Gregory Peter Nybo, who passed away during the final editing of this book. Not only was he a caring father and a wise man, he was a writer, a teacher, and was the catalyst for this book. Thanks dad ; -) we miss you!

Contents

Foreword   Alison Cooke Mintzer   vii

Acknowledgments   ix

Introduction   xiii

Chapter 1   Retirement Readiness: The Super
             Savers and the Ill-Prepared   1

Chapter 2   A Brief History of Retirement   19

Chapter 3   State of the Union   31

Chapter 4   Rise of the DC Plan   43

Chapter 5   Financial Literacy   57

Chapter 6   Lessons Learned, Changing Outcomes   71

Chapter 7   The Power of Context   85

Chapter 8   Beliefs and Resolve   103

Chapter 9   Tell Me a Story   121

Chapter 10   Join the Dance   133

Chapter 11   Letters to Stakeholders   143

Bibliography   153

Glossary   161

List of Contributors   167

Index   175

About the Authors   185

Foreword

We often hear, and use, the phrase "retire with dignity." According to the Oxford English dictionary, dignity means "the quality or state of being worthy, honored, or esteemed." I believe therefore that to retire with dignity is doing so with more than just the minimum needed to get by. It is doing so with a certain level of self-respect, being able to maintain the necessities, at a minimum, and hopefully able to afford a few niceties as well.

As a fellow member of the retirement industry, one who has spent much of his career learning and understanding what is—and is not—happening in the world of retirement savings, Stig Nybo believes the same thing. In these pages, he presents a call to action to encourage all to help Americans secure their retirement. *Transform Tomorrow* helps put clarity around the questions: what exactly do we mean by a dignified retirement, and how are we helping—and can we help—Americans get there?

Only by knowing where we have come from can we move forward. These pages provide a context of how our retirement plan, and 401(k) system, got to where it is today, and identify the misconceptions that Americans must overcome to understand how best to move forward.

For example, why is 65 the traditional retirement age, and were Americans so much better off years ago with defined benefit (traditional pension) plans? Although I grew up seeing both of my grandfathers end their careers having worked for one company most of their decades of employment—providing them with full pensions—that actually was not the experience of many. Job hopping is not a new phenomenon, and for all the talk about the "death" of pensions, in fact, Stig points out, coverage of Americans by retirement plans is actually more common now.

And yet we are faced with a dismal savings rate, longevity increases that might lead to people spending more time in retirement than they did working, and a lack of financial education and literacy.

Where will this lack of savings get us? As one adviser to retirement plans often notes in her preretiree seminars, there is a lot more cat food sold in Florida than there are cats to eat it. Now, that is a somewhat disturbing—and perhaps hyperbolic—example, but it is true that a lack of savings can mean even the most basic needs are threatened.

Therefore, as *Transform Tomorrow* says, we need a national initiative to change that. By recognizing this massive social issue and putting the right context around it, Stig has created a message not just for the retirement industry, but for the country as a whole.

With the close to 10 years I have spent affiliated with Asset International, the publisher of *PLANSPONSOR* and *PLANADVISER*, publications focused on helping companies and advisers provide the best retirement programs they can to employees, I firmly believe that what we do matters. Helping companies offer a retirement savings vehicle to their employees is often the only way an American will begin to think about retirement savings.

However, as the years have gone on, I have been acutely aware that the messages that we focus on are all for nothing if we don't get one message right—the need to save. As an industry, we've spent a lot of time and money trying to make Americans investors, instead of making them savers, and I do think that those of us who know better should be able to help those who don't.

As I constantly reiterate to members of my staff, I believe this is one of the largest social and public policy issues of our time. Regardless of what industry you work in and what position you hold, it is incumbent upon those of us who are aware of this issue to get behind this savings campaign initiative and do what each of us can to *Transform Tomorrow*.

Alison Cooke Mintzer
Global Editor-in-Chief, *PLANSPONSOR*,
PLANADVISER, PLANSPONSOR Europe
Asset International, Inc.
New York, NY

Acknowledgments

When things got tough an old friend of mine would ask me, "Stig, how do you eat an elephant?" And then, before I could answer, he would always reply to his own question with a smile, "One bite at a time." This has always made sense to me, and it is essentially how this book was written, one bite at a time. But as they say, the real truth often runs a little deeper and is found somewhere below the surface. If asked that same question today, my answer would be a bit different; it would simply be, "Not alone." Why? Because in my 50 years, I've never accomplished anything worthwhile without a lot of help from others. This book was no exception.

While I take full credit for the desire to write this book and for my belief that it was (and is) sorely needed, I fully share the credit for the knowledge within its covers with those who contributed so freely to its contents. Over the course of its writing we consulted with many knowledgeable and passionate individuals who opened their hearts and minds to our cause as only a 401(k) Whisperer—a term that will gain clarity as you read on—could. While their names are not mentioned here, they are listed in the final pages of this text, along with a short list of their accomplishments. I am truly grateful for their contribution, without which this book would not have been written.

But it doesn't only take knowledge to write a book, it takes a huge commitment. And while the credit for that commitment is often adorned on the author, it really belongs to all of those willing souls that get sucked into the vortex; and I'm not sure there's any other way to describe it. What's really perplexing is how utterly willing they all were (and are) to dig in and not for pay, but on their own time, on weekends and evenings. I've finally come to realize that it's just who they are as human beings. They believe deeply, as I do, in the cause of retirement readiness and are willing to put their talents to work and sacrifice time and energy to make a difference. I am humbled by their enthusiasm and their contribution, so please bear with me as I pay what little respect I can in these few pages.

I've always maintained that it takes a whole lot more talent to create, than edit (with no disrespect intended to my editors). It is with this in mind that I sincerely thank those who helped contribute to the actual writing of this book. To Patricia Advaney, Julie Quinlan, and Charlie Avallone: it was truly an unfair request to ask that you be clairvoyant enough to understand my intent and direction and write the content you actually did, and then to be subject to the violent strokes of the editing pen as the tone was refined and content changed. I am truly grateful for your time and talent.

While we've tried to tone down the technical content to the point of being tolerable for all our readers, our topic simply cannot be done justice without addressing some facts, figures, and technical jargon. A big thank-you goes to Patti Rowey and Catherine Collinson who provided research and technical support; to Heidi Cho who wrote the glossary; and to Jolene Crittenden who wrote the bibliography. To Alison Cooke Mintzer, thank you for your thoughtful words in our Foreword. And to Greg Miller-Breetz, thank you for ensuring we had our legal i's dotted and t's crossed.

To my proofreaders—Jonathan Anderson, Charlie Avallone, Catherine Collinson, Jeanne de Cervens, Jim Douglas, Pat Kendall, Monica Mitchell, Julie Quinlan and Patti Rowey—your careful work is indeed appreciated. But more importantly, your ability to deliver the message without shooting the messenger will forever be noted. As all of us who have ever written can attest, there is a little bit of our soul in every word, and I've come to believe that red is just an abusive color (at least as it relates to edits). Thank you for your kind but honest delivery.

To Amy Haley—someone who you will all have the pleasure of meeting in the text of this book because of her willingness to share— thank you for openly sharing your Super Saver ways. You are truly an inspiration to all of us who have saved too little and a glimmer of hope that we can right this ship, if not for ourselves, then for those generations yet to come. And to Mathew Frost, thank you for being an inspiration to our kids and for being willing to share your story on how you are spreading financial literacy. Oh, and thank you for being a teacher to begin with.

To Kent Callahan and Peter Kunkel, thank you from the bottom of my heart for letting me run with this project and for supporting it from day one. Thank you to Dave Shute and Barbara Muir for buying in early and staying with me throughout the ups and downs of this arduous process, and to Jason Crane and Deb Rubin, for so eloquently putting theory into practice as we take our message to the world. You are very much a part of what we have created. A very special thank you goes to Jolene Crittenden, who was the quarterback of this endeavor. Jolene, you are such a unique talent and have the ability to help others get more out of themselves than they could ever possibly get without you. As with so many things in my world, this wouldn't have happened without you.

To Liz Alexander, my co-author, it has been a wild ride, hasn't it? I'd be lying if I said I've enjoyed every minute of this journey; at times I've wondered what the heck I was thinking when I took it on. I'm pretty sure I've run the gambit of emotion, from elation to despair, and back again. But boy, has it been a worthwhile ride! You have been professional, insightful, firm, challenging, and just a joy to work with. What we produced together is far greater than anything I could have produced on my own—Thank You! Now please don't take offense, but I'm sure glad it's done.

To my dad, Greg, and to Margaret; to my mom, Tove; and to the Austin clan: my brother Dag and his family, Claudia, Mikael, Selvia, and Claudia; and to my close friends—thank you all for your support and enthusiasm. But more importantly, I'm sorry for being missing in action over the last year. Your patience with my absence has been duly noted and much appreciated. And a special callout to my coach and brother, Dag, who simply said, "What are you waiting for? Go ahead and write that book!" Unbelievably, it happened!

Finally, to my remarkable wife Holly, and my two precious boys, Andreas and Torsten: Boy, do I owe you big! During a normal year, you guys make more sacrifices than I have a right to ask for. But this last year was truly above and beyond reasonableness. I've missed events, games, and family outings, all in the name of this project. This extra duty came on top of an already rigorous schedule, and you guys have been the balancing item—you are awesome! My sincere hope is that this book will be the catalyst for people to have a different, more productive conversation about saving for retirement and that it will make a difference to society. I also hope that it sets a small example that you can do anything you put your mind to. I love you with all my heart and always remember these words we've read so many times . . . "And will you succeed? Yes! You will, indeed! (98 and 3/4 percent guaranteed.) KID, YOU'LL MOVE MOUNTAINS!"—Dr. Seuss.

Introduction

The crying Indian campaign, premiering on Earth Day 1971, had it all: a heart-wrenching central figure, an appeal to mythic America, and a catchy slogan.

—*Orion* magazine article

On January 1, 1969, President Richard M. Nixon took office as the new President of the United States of America with a promise to achieve peace with honor and withdraw a half million U.S. troops from Vietnam.

Yet two years later, the United States was still embroiled in war. At that time, protests were commonplace, with 350,000 veterans marching on Washington, DC and San Francisco, and 50,000 demonstrators setting up camp in Washington, DC's Algonquin Peace City. The free speech, free love, and peace movement was in full swing across the country. I was nine and growing up in the epicenter of controversy: Berkeley, California.

That same year, the UN's Secretary General U Thant announced that Earth Day would become an annual celebration, wishing that " . . . there only be peaceful and cheerful Earth Days to come for our beautiful Spaceship Earth, as it continues to spin and circle in frigid space with its warm and fragile cargo of animate life."

The origins of Earth Day can be traced back to then-U.S. Senator Gaylord Nelson, who had pledged to focus on environmental issues in order to, as he put it, "stem the tide of environmental disaster."

In a climate ripe for environmental activism, 1971 saw the use of DDT outlawed by the U.S. Court of Appeals; Ralph Nader formed his Earth Act group; the United States formally ceased commercial whaling; and Greenpeace was born in Vancouver, Canada. Change was in the air. Surprisingly, despite my young age, it was for me, too.

Iron Eyes Cody

We all have memories that for one reason or another are indelibly etched into our subconscious, typically only surfacing during brief periods of adult nostalgia. They are invariably linked to emotionally impactful events, like the assassination of JFK or the *Challenger* disaster. Although I didn't realize it at the time, one such memory was formed for me on Earth Day, 1971.

Truthfully, I don't remember much about that day; it was a long time ago. Nevertheless the following two events that occurred, neither one of them overtly sensational, somehow became a permanent part of who I am.

I don't remember whom I was with, what car I was in, or even where we were going. I don't even remember being consciously aware of what I was seeing at the time. It wasn't until later that things fell into place. We were on the Bayshore Freeway in the San Francisco Bay Area, and I was looking out the window, most likely in an effort to distract myself from feeling carsick. My eyes drifted to the mud flats of the bay and took in the debris. Half-buried tires stood upright in the mud and trash littered the wetlands. I remember an old rusting carcass of a car sitting in the mud, at what seemed like a hundred yards from the shore, and wondering how it got there. A large bird was perched on the roof, a Blue Heron, which is why I believe that this image stuck in my memory. Looking back, the strange thing was that this blight on an otherwise beautiful landscape seemed quite normal.

Later that evening, while my brother and I were watching *Alias Smith and Jones* on the family's black-and-white TV set, the network switched to the inevitable commercial break. A steady, almost hypnotic drumbeat captured my attention. On the screen a canoe came into view with a Native American man on board. The camera changed perspective and the Indian—having pulled his canoe onto a rocky beach strewn with debris—was now standing by the side of a busy highway, massive towers belching grey smoke in the background. The music intensified as a bag of trash, thrown from a car window, exploded at his feet. Then a deep voice said, "Some people have a deep abiding respect for the beauty that was once this country . . . and some people don't." As the scene ended, the camera zoomed in on the Native American's face as a single tear rolled down his cheek.

Regardless of when you were born, you are probably familiar with the Crying Indian Public Service Announcement (PSA), which went on to become one of the top advertising campaigns of the twentieth century. The actor used in the campaign was known as Iron Eyes Cody and, although born to parents originally from Sicily, he had played Native Americans in Hollywood films for years. In 1995 Iron Eyes Cody was even honored by the American Indian community for bringing attention to and helping to promote their cause. Forty years later, a YouTube search for "Crying Indian" nets multiple versions of the original commercial with hit rates numbering hundreds of thousands each. Viewers have rated this PSA: "The best commercial ever," "Best PSA ever made," and "Powerful."

As one of the initiatives launched by the nonprofit organization Keep America Beautiful, which had been founded in 1953, the Iron Eyes Cody media campaign had a profound impact on American beliefs, values, and behavior around littering. As you'll discover in a later chapter, thanks to this and other efforts, the overall litter count has been reduced by 61 percent since 1969.

There is no doubt in my mind that the emotionally charged, clear, and immediately understood message promoted by the Crying Indian, supported by legislation and community action, helped to completely transform our national landscape. Suddenly the trash I saw earlier that day, which was blighting the Bayshore Freeway, took on a different meaning. Even as a child, I distinctly remember feeling—as a consequence of seeing that TV commercial—that littering was wrong and we needed to do something to change things.

Retirement Readiness

On the surface, the issues of saving for retirement and environmental pollution may appear to have little in common. Yet today there exists a similar sense, nascent perhaps but growing, that we need to do something about retirement readiness and provoke people to save more, in the same way that we changed our perspectives about the environment and littering.

What sparked the desire to write this book was a simple but profound question: what will it take to ensure a broader, sustainable sense of retirement readiness in America? In order to answer that question, we sought the perspectives of a wide range of experts. We interviewed them at length to gather their opinions on the current workplace retirement savings system, financial literacy, our resolve to tackle this problem head on, and what might be the message we could use to rally everyone around this issue, similar to the way the Crying Indian helped to clean up the American landscape.

This was never a question I felt capable of answering on my own, despite having worked in the retirement services industry for the past two decades—first as a financial advisor and more recently as President of Pension Sales and Distribution at Transamerica Retirement Solutions. Nor is it a question I believe other industry professionals, or even policymakers, should try to address on their own. Even if we feel as if these are the fields on which the battle is being fought right now, it may not be where the war will be won or even where the best ideas will be found.

Some of the smartest organizations—ranging from the InnoCentive initiative backed by the likes of Booz Allen Hamilton, Eli Lilly, and Procter & Gamble to Google's Solve for X—are opening up challenges to seemingly insurmountable problems to people with different ways of thinking and different skill sets.

Why? Because, as the Founder of the World Innovation Institute, Naveen Jain, points out in a *Forbes* article subtitled "Why Non-Experts Are Better at Disruptive Innovation": "I believe that the best ideas come from those not immersed in the details of a particular field. Experts, far too often, engage in a kind of *myopic thinking*. Those who are down in the weeds are likely to miss the big picture."

Similarly, we believe the problem of retirement readiness will likely be solved by existing and new sources of creativity, with people coming together to uncover new solutions and a way forward.

Those of us involved in the effort to drive retirement readiness (for example, industry professionals, policymakers, and employers who sponsor retirement plans), may be suffering from a similar challenge: we have been so close to this issue for so long that we need to broaden our thinking in order to find true solutions, possibly including how we define the concept we call retirement. After all, as you will discover when we outline the history of retirement in the United States in Chapter 2, there has never truly been a cohesive vision around the issue of retirement; this was apparent long before there *was* a retirement services industry. This is a societal problem and we need to pull together as a society to fix it! Fresh minds on the issue of retirement readiness are definitely required to help build the right kind of campaign that ensures everyone who wants to or needs to can enjoy a retirement that's fully funded.

Ironically, there are plenty of national campaigns concerned with promoting health and extending our lives, like healthy eating, ending obesity, and learning to look after our hearts—but nothing focused on making sure we all have enough money in order to enjoy living those extra years. Why is that, we wanted to know? If Iron Eyes Cody could help change our culture around littering, why do we not have a similar campaign aimed at ensuring retirement readiness today?

The Crying Indian PSA was both timeless and a product of its time. From a timeless perspective (and we urge you to watch the commercial first, if you're not already aware of it), the genius was that it touched everyone individually and collectively. Even as a young boy, I felt the message that Iron Eyes Cody conveyed, with that single tear, was being directed specifically at me. At the same time, there was a feeling of solidarity—of collective responsibility—that also emanated from it. The villains were some hypothetical "them," not us, even though collectively we were polluting the landscape. The Iron Eyes Cody spots achieved that delicate balance between galvanizing people to take action while at the same time not pointing a wagging finger at us for having caused the problem in the first place. (That's not to say there wasn't plenty of criticism aimed at the campaign, but that's an issue we'll address later in this book.)

Aside from its modern mythological quality—of tapping into universal human emotions and values—the campaign was also very much of its time. As mentioned earlier, there was considerable social unrest and a spirit of rebellion in the air; the country was experiencing a stagnating economy and America was embroiled in a highly charged war with no obvious exit strategy. The parallels between then and now are quite striking. Simply swap the Occupation of Alcatraz for Occupy Wall Street, Vietnam for Afghanistan or Iraq, and Stagflation for the Great Recession!

For any message to succeed, regardless of how powerfully it taps into our emotions or how brilliantly it is executed, the environment needs to be right. Nineteen seventy-one was obviously the right time for the Crying Indian campaign and we believe that 2013 and beyond is ripe for launching a similar message around retirement readiness and financial security.

Forty years ago we began tackling the blight of littering and pollution in this country, and while that is an ongoing battle, you just have to look outside your window and compare that to memories such as the one I described earlier to see how far we've come. Today, can we effect the same culture change with respect to how much and when we begin to plan and save for retirement?

This is not just a book but a clarion call to start a movement, whose purpose it is to provoke everyone (by which we mean the American worker, policymakers, retirement services professionals, employers, and the media) to get behind a campaign that will fundamentally change the way we view retirement readiness.

Mapping Out the Chapters

Rather than attempt to provide the right answers, we are deliberately setting out to ask what we believe to be the right questions. The conversation, in its broadest sense, hasn't really heated up yet. After all, chances are that *you* haven't participated in the way we are proposing!

In order to help you better understand and potentially reframe this issue, we open the first chapter by asking why human beings aren't better at making long-term decisions. If we accept that we are all getting older and one day we will no longer be willing or able to work, why is it that we don't plan earlier and better for our retirement years?

Rather than paint the typical doom-and-gloom picture, however, we also want to identify who is retirement ready, and highlight what one survey has named the Super Savers—individuals who, for one reason or another, have confidently set enough money aside to retire even earlier than the norm. We then contrast these with the vast majority of people in this country, those who are ill-prepared.

On any journey, it is vital to plot two points: where you are now and where you are headed. In some cases, it is also helpful to review the direction from which you have come. For that reason, Chapter 2 takes a backward look at the history of this notion we call retirement and its economic, political, and social implications from the beginning of the nineteenth century through to the emergence of what are called defined benefit plans. Not least, we outline that one thing we have never had, not even today, is a cohesive vision for this country around retirement readiness, a vision that both inspires and unites us.

In shaping Chapter 3, entitled State of the Union, we went back in time once more. On this occasion, we journeyed to a point when the whole of America was indeed inspired and united behind a compelling vision—that of the NASA space program, as articulated by former President John F. Kennedy. This chapter reviews the near-catastrophe that was the Apollo 13 mission and asks: What kind of command-control team do we have in place with respect to ensuring a safe touchdown for citizens during their retirement years? And what kind of system infrastructure supports the effort?

If you were to ask the average person about the pension system and how it has evolved over the past 50 years, the story would sound something like this: It used to be that we worked for one company for our entire lives and then retired with a full pension; employees were loyal and employers paternalistic. In Chapter 4, we address this misperception head-on as we investigate how the modern pension has evolved. We review the retirement plan system as well as the risks associated with managing retirement plans (both defined benefit plans and defined contribution plans) and how those risks have morphed over time.

After illustrating how the risks associated with retirement savings shifted from the employer offering a defined benefit plan to the individual, whose retirement savings now rests largely with a defined contribution plan, we also ask how prepared is the American worker for this newfound responsibility, given the current state of financial literacy in the United States? Chapter 5 focuses on the extent to which the average American is realistically equipped to make the investment decisions they are now being called upon to make with respect to their workplace savings plans. It asks: what does it mean to be "financially literate"?

Having outlined the main issues that got us where we are today, we change direction in Chapter 6 to look at what we can learn from a number of highly successful behavior change advertising campaigns, ones that might help inform how a nationally supported retirement readiness campaign could be designed. Specifically, we identify two behavior change concepts that fall along a continuum: with context on one end and beliefs on the other.

Chapter 7 further explores the first of those concepts—context. It identifies that while this does indeed drive results in terms of changing peoples' behavior (such as how more easily accessible trash cans help reduce littering), without a clear vision guiding us, the results we get are not necessarily the ones we want.

In Chapter 8 we tackle the other side of this equation—beliefs and resolve. When it comes to our self-efficacy beliefs around retirement (meaning the extent to which we believe we are personally capable of adopting new behaviors, such as saving earlier and deferring more money into plans), do Americans really have what it takes to make this change? Or, as we heard over and over from many of our interviewees, are we more of a spending culture that believes that if our consumerism were to take a back seat to savings, then we would detrimentally impact the U.S. economy? This chapter looks at our resolve to fundamentally shift course on the issue of retirement readiness from the perspectives of the individual American worker, plan sponsors (employers), the retirement services industry, and policymakers.

If we were to assume that every one of these stakeholders resolved to get behind a unifying message, what might that campaign look like? In order to help inform the creation of a straw man campaign, in Chapter 9 we investigate what it takes to craft a compelling, "sticky" message using age-old storytelling techniques. How was it, for example, that Florence Nightingale single-handedly transformed the medical profession? Why do the "founded in a garage" myths abound in high-tech start-ups? And what helped two former college sweethearts transform Uglydoll from a private gesture to a worldwide toy phenomenon?

The Final Question . . . For Now

Despite the best efforts of the retirement services industry, the average American is still not saving enough to retire comfortably. What we believe is needed is a nationally recognized, coordinated retirement readiness campaign along the lines of successful Public Service Announcements—like Iron Eyes Cody and Rosie the Riveter—that will help to change behavior and reshape the culture of our nation.

This book began as an initial call to action for such a campaign and we could have left it there. But we didn't. In Chapter 10 we offer an invitation to participate in a coalition of stakeholders around a philosophy of "Yes, and . . . ?" Plus, we are making significant investments of time and money in funding a web presence, as a first step toward attracting those creative thinkers who can help design a straw man campaign, as part of the movement to change the way America saves.

Whether you are an actual (or would-be) retirement plan participant, an employer with a current retirement plan or intention to initiate one, a financial advisor or other member of the retirement services community, or a policymaker—there is an open letter at the close of this book with your name on it! Each of these messages outlines the key responsibilities we feel you need to accept in order to contribute to the outcome we are seeking to bring about. Our aim with these letters is to provoke and inspire you. We need to wake up and consider the different ways in which we can commit to taking action around a goal relevant to the constituency to which we belong. But beyond that, to help build a coalition in which all constituencies come together in order to make real progress around this issue of retirement readiness. We desperately need to do that, because if we do *nothing* we will fail not just ourselves and not just ourselves, but our children and future generations.

There were many things told to us during the course of interviewing people for this book that were impactful and profound. One that especially resonated was this comment by Charlie Ruffel, President of Kudu Advisors and founder of *PLANSPONSOR*® magazine, who said:

> *At the end of the day, an absolute hallmark of a civilized society is for someone to be able, after decades of work, to retire with financial dignity.*

My question to you, then, as you read this book is: how do we make that happen?

Stig Nybo
Portola Valley, California
September 2012

Chapter 1

Retirement Readiness: The Super Savers and the Ill-Prepared

Never doubt that a small group of thoughtful, committed citizens can change the world; indeed, it's the only thing that ever has.
— Margaret Mead, American anthropologist

It is one of those questions that psychologists and economists love (and live) to grapple with: why do we so frequently fail to act in our long-term best interests?

For example, take a common situation at the organizational level. Findings from Burson-Marsteller's 2011 Crisis Preparedness study showed that while 79 percent of business decision makers believed they were only 12 months away from a potential business crisis event, and while they recognized the risk such events posed to both revenues and reputation, just over half of the companies polled (54 percent) admitted to having a crisis preparedness plan in place. Of those who did, two-thirds agreed that it was probably inadequate.

At an individual level, we have a similar situation with respect to retirement readiness. According to The Investment Company Institute (ICI), "the average balance of Americans' 401(k) accounts was just over $60,000 at the end of 2010." This means that aside from traditional pension plans (typically known as defined benefit (DB) plans, which only 19 percent of private sector workers participate in) and Social Security (which many Americans expect will provide lower benefits in the future), the average American currently has $60,000 to last them throughout their retirement years. According to ICI, "this low 401(k) plan balance is alarming," but it doesn't take an expert to come to that conclusion.

The good news is that when we narrow our view to specifically look at individuals who are in their 60s and are approaching retirement and then expand our focus to include both IRAs and 401(k) balances, the picture changes substantially. According to EBRI's 2010 integrated defined contribution/IRA database, their combined balance at the end of 2010 stood at $275,517. In the spirit of full disclosure, the analysis was limited to individuals with both 401(k) and IRA balances at the end of 2010, but does demonstrate the emerging success of defined contribution (DC) plans. While this is significantly better than the previously mentioned $60,000 average 401(k) balance, there is still considerable work to be done.

Just how much savings are enough for today's soon-to-be-retired Boomers (individuals born between 1946 and 1964) is an issue we will address shortly. But think about it this way. Life expectancy has increased by almost 30 years in the last century and if retirement age remains in the mid-sixties, it could soon be the case that today's Millennials (also known as the Echo Boomers, Generation Y, or Net Generation—those people born between 1980 and 2000) will need to save enough money to cover them for as many retirement years as the number of years they were in employment. The longer they take to start saving, the harder it will be for them to make up that shortfall.

Who is promoting *that* message?

The level of personal responsibility involved in being prepared to retire when you choose, whether that means stopping work altogether, working part-time, or perhaps venturing into later-life entrepreneurialism, is taking its time to seep into our national consciousness.

Gallagher Retirement Service's Mike DiCenso told us that just five years ago, 80 percent of people surveyed said they thought they had enough money saved for retirement and expected to be "very comfortable," despite the fact that the average 401(k) account balance stood at that time at just $67,000. Even if there had been ironclad guarantees of high investment returns over the years that followed, that still would have likely produced a balance insufficient for them to retire.

Let us look at the example of a participant who has accumulated as much as $250,000 by the time they retire. Using conventional wisdom, a 4 percent withdrawal rate has generally been accepted as the amount a retiree can withdraw annually from their account and still have money to last them through retirement. That means a balance of $250,000 nets a retiree approximately $10,000 a year, or $833 a month. Now, consider the individual with an account balance of just $67,000. Using that same 4 percent assumption, that is an income of $2,680 a year, or $223 a month. As DiCenso pointed out, "At that time it wasn't making sense to us how so many people felt that they would be ready for retirement." His comments become even more relevant considering the past few years of tumultuous stock market performance and the current state of low interest rates, which bring even the 4 percent rule into serious question.

So, back to our opening question: Why don't intelligent, responsible human beings connect their current behavior with future consequences?

You could blame this on the Paleomammalian hardware that has managed our fight or flight responses since the dawn of humankind. Specifically, those neural structures known as the amygdalae, which Daniel Pink referred to in *A Whole New Mind: Why Right-Brainers Will Rule the Future* as "the brain's Department of Homeland Security." In times of heightened threat these little almond-shaped regions of the brain (the word amygdala means almond in Greek) are on high alert, constantly on the lookout for danger. When we are overly busy, mentally processing all the emotions associated with challenges ranging from mounting credit card debt and possible home repossession to the implications of the Great Recession and the War on Terror, there is very little bandwidth left to focus on the future and how we desire it to be different than the present. But this avoidance behavior is not new and the full explanation for our lack of planning likely runs much deeper than our reactions to recent events.

Joe Mrozek, Managing Director and Head of Middle Markets, Bank of America Merrill Lynch, characterizes the challenge as a tortoise and hare phenomenon. "There is no magic and nothing exciting about retirement planning. In reality, it's just a slow grind throughout your working lifetime. The most successful people are the methodical savers that make a consistent commitment to an investment program and stick with it through the ups and downs." When stated in these straightforward terms, could this be why it's difficult to engage the average person to save for retirement?

Nevertheless, some people are highly successful at focusing on the future. Later in this chapter we will introduce you to a cohort of Super Savers known as the Future Early Retirees, identified by the Transamerica Center for Retirement Studies®, a nonprofit, private foundation, as doing everything they can to maintain their own personal vision for a bright, post-working future.

Many people's emotional states remain in overdrive, however— not just from fear and anxiety, but from regret at the opportunities they feel they have missed.

This is not just a U.S. phenomenon. For example, a recent www .plansponsor.com article reported how Canadian Baby Boomers regretted failing to plan earlier and better for their retirement. Forty-two percent said they wished they had started saving at an earlier age; a quarter of people polled said they regretted not making regular contributions and maximizing the contributions they were allowed to make; slightly fewer (24 percent) said they should have given more thought to, and budgeted more for, their retirement years than they did.

Over on our side of the border, we Americans are grappling with plenty of emotions of our own. The National Institute on Retirement Security (NIRS) study entitled *Pensions and Retirement Security 2011: A Roadmap for Policymakers* reported the highly anxious state of most Americans, 84 percent of whom are concerned about the current economic conditions affecting their ability to achieve a secure retirement.

A Comfortable Retirement

But, what does it mean to be retirement ready?

Given all the variables we need to compute—from how long we are likely to live, how healthy we will be during our later years, and how much health care costs will drain the savings we do have—how do we even begin to get a handle on how much we need to save, even if we have the time and disposable income to do so? After all, we don't live in a world such as the one depicted by the 1976 movie *Logan's Run,* in which the inhabitants had a known number of years to live and a crystal embedded in their hands that turned black to indicate that their human shelf life had expired! In reality, we never know when we are going to die, or what kind of health we can expect to enjoy (or not) during our later years. With all the variables involved, how can anyone expect to plan effectively for retirement? (We will look at the issue of longevity risk more closely later in the book.)

What kind of comfortable retirement are we expecting in any case? Perhaps bowed by the onslaught of recent financial crises that have given the Boomer generation, especially, a major wake-up call, it appears that the average American today does not have unrealistically high expectations. While the marketing of retirement in the late 1950s and early 1960s stressed the appeal of foreign travel and otherwise glamorized these later years, as we outline in Chapter 3, definitions of a financially secure retirement from the same NIRS study cited earlier included such practical, day-to-day considerations as:

◆ Maintaining a home and not having to worry about paying for it.
◆ Having adequate medical care and coverage.
◆ Being able to pay bills and address other family responsibilities.

While these are laudably pragmatic views, they don't account for two vitally important aspects of retirement readiness. In addition to having the right replacement ratio (the percentage of current income that you would need in retirement to maintain your current standard of living), you must also have sufficient knowledge and resolve to make the savings you do have last.

As is evidenced by the NIRS findings cited earlier, few Americans appear to be thinking along the lines recommended by UBS Financial Services' Paul D'Aiutolo. He advises plan participants not to even *think* about retiring until they have no mortgage payment, no credit card debt, and no adult children or grandchildren living under their care for whom they are responsible for big-ticket items like a college education. When they've significantly reduced or eradicated those debts, says D'Aiutolo, they can much more reasonably expect to cover their expenses in retirement. But (and it's a big but), as D'Aiutolo points out, "What we have as a country right now is very different than in the past.

We're not only asking retirement plans to replace 80 percent of income, we're asking them to replace income that is still needed to support mortgages, adult children, credit cards and things that were never intended by the original retirement system, because we didn't even have credit then to the extent that we do now."

According to an analysis of data provided by the Bureau of Labor Statistics, the average American centenarian (a person who lives to be 100 years old) can expect to spend around $3.5 million in his or her lifetime. Between the ages of 50 and 81—which is the average life expectancy of most 50-year-olds today—we are likely to run up bills totaling $1.4 million. Of course this assumes living to our average life expectancy! What if we end up living to be 91, or even 100?

As Charles Passy commented in *The Cost of Living Longer—Much Longer*, "Call it the new death calculus: the twenty-first century equation for determining human longevity. Or call it misguided guesswork, as some critics have. Either way, it's hard to imagine a math problem that has flummoxed humanity for longer. (Actuaries, in fact, have been fumbling for an answer since 1583, when the first life insurance policy was issued.) And it's even harder to conceive of one with more at stake in the outcome."

If living to be 100 years old sounds like it will only be a problem for a tiny minority, consider this: the United States and Japan are the countries with the highest percentages of centenarians. It has been estimated that in the United States alone, the number of 100-year-olds will rise from the current 75,000 to over 600,000 by the middle of the century. In just a few years' time (2017 to be precise) we will celebrate a remarkable first: more people in the United States who are 65 and over than children younger than five.

Saving for a time when our ability to earn is diminished, assuming we want to continue working at all, coupled with increasing costs of health care that could stretch for 20 years or more is, as Laura L. Carstensen pointed out in *Retirement in an Era of Long Life*, "a tall order." According to one report, people in their eighties spend 57 percent more on health insurance than their counterparts who are in their fifties (Marte 2012). Whether we are prepared for it or not, that's part of the reality of being retirement ready in the twenty-first century.

As we have discovered, among America's current 1.9 million nonagenarians (people who live into their 90s), these individuals rely heavily on Social Security payments and pensions. Concerns about the ability of Social Security to meet its obligations for future generations are beyond the scope of this book. What is of direct concern, however, is the number of Americans who, for one reason or another, do not participate in any kind of retirement savings or pension plans.

Typically, lower-income households are less likely to save for retirement, for reasons that are likely obvious. They are also more likely to have "just getting by" as their greatest financial priority. While Social Security, as it stands currently, does replace a higher percentage of lifetime earnings for lower as opposed to higher-income earners, complete reliance on Social Security is not appropriate for any American.

Also, part of this issue is the fact that the norms of lifecycle consumption mean that most workers do not begin to save for retirement until they are well into their working careers, their primary focus earlier being funding their education, buying homes and cars, and keeping a certain level of cash on hand to pay for emergency needs.

For lower and middle-income earners, not having the money to save was typically cited as the reason not to participate in a defined contribution plan, although for the middle-income earners, other reasons included having a spouse with a plan or simply not thinking about it (Holden 2011). Acting like an ostrich with its head in the sand could be a costly mistake—one that many Americans have made and continue to make.

In the same article cited earlier, Passy points out that simply adding another four years of life to current projections would require an additional $160,000 of retirement savings to maintain even a modest lifestyle—which puts the current $60,000 average retirement balance into stark perspective. Whose retirement strategies are likely to remain unaffected? According to Stephen C. Goss, the chief actuary of the Social Services Administration, it is someone like Bill Gates with unlimited means.

Introducing the Super Savers

It is not all doom and gloom, however. There is a significant group of people we term Super Savers who are doing everything possible not just to be comfortable when they retire, but to actively lower the age at which they choose to do so. These Future Early Retirees exhibit characteristics that have helped us to identify the habits that need to be highlighted in any campaign designed to stress the importance of retirement readiness—if not for Baby Boomers, then at least for the generations that follow them.

In 2011, the Transamerica Center for Retirement Studies (TCRS) discovered a hidden cohort of Super Savers within the data of its Twelfth Annual Transamerica Retirement Survey. These findings were released in a report entitled *A Source of Inspiration: Future Early Retirees*. This Super Saver group isn't especially privileged or affluent; they're mostly your average Joe or Jane (the *Millionaire Next Door*), who realize that if you want to control, rather than be controlled by, life's circumstances, it helps to have a plan in place.

Much of what is described in that report applies to Amy Haley, one of our interviewees who, at the age of 26, has been saving for retirement since the age of 18 and contributes between 10 and 20 percent of her earnings every month.

Describing herself as a compulsive saver since childhood, when her medium was a piggy bank rather than a 401(k) plan, Amy admits to being heavily influenced by her grandfather with respect to the way he invested and managed his money. Formerly a teacher and later an engineer after going back to college, Amy's grandfather died leaving his widow with the ability to live comfortably off of his considerable savings.

Amy's behavior is similar to that of the Future Early Retirees cited by TCRS who always chose to participate in whatever retirement plans their employers had made available, started to save early in life (median age 25), and exhibited a greater propensity to be involved in managing and monitoring their retirement accounts. This behavior is in stark contrast with most of her peer group, however.

Says Amy:

I have peers here who are five, six, seven, ten years older than me and know far less about what it really means to contribute any amount of money to a retirement plan, and why it's important. They don't see an immediate benefit and they have never taken the time to educate themselves about it.

When you're hired on, we have a meeting with HR to sign up for insurance and benefits and things of that nature, so we only get a one-time exposure.

We do have a financial advisor who comes to speak with us roughly once a month. But you have to schedule an appointment with him and you kind of have to take some initiative to seek out answers from him.

I guess if we really want to push for more people to be more knowledgeable on the subject, companies should not assume that they are going to seek out those resources or educate themselves, because that's not been my experience.

As the nineteenth century "father of psychology" William James once pronounced, "All our life . . . is but a mass of habits." Trying to unpack all the psychological and other variables as to why some people, like Amy Haley, make better preparations for their long-term security than others—even if that were possible—would make anyone's head spin. What is possible, and we attempt to do in this book, is to align our understanding of people's habits, their behaviors, and their beliefs, with support from all stakeholders: employers, the retirement industry, policymakers, the media, as well as the average American worker, so that preparing for retirement can become more routine and automatic.

How? As the *New York Times's* Charles Duhigg points out in his book *The Power of Habit: Why We Do What We Do in Life and Business*, in order to get into the "habit loop" we need a "keystone habit that creates a culture." One example was the way pioneering advertising genius Claude C. Hopkins sold toothpaste to the American public back in the early years of the twentieth century.

Brushing one's teeth, at least daily, was not a social norm for most Americans back in those days. But Hopkins, understanding the power of habit modification and its link to rewards, was determined to promote (and hence sell for his client) a new toothpaste brand called Pepsodent. He did so by not only highlighting the advantage of having a beautiful smile, but stressing the great-tasting feeling that comes from brushing your teeth regularly. Once Americans had gotten into the habit of brushing their teeth and experiencing the difference for themselves, missing even one day just didn't feel right. Note that what

Hopkins knew—as do all superior advertising geniuses—is that we buy into a message more because of feelings and emotions than we do from rational argument. Unfortunately most of what we do in the retirement services industry has to do with the latter.

Of course, a one-time message is never enough. Undoubtedly regular, catchy advertising messages like "You'll wonder where the yellow went when you brush your teeth with Pepsodent" provided the necessary trigger—or cues—that prompted Americans decades ago to adopt what is now a daily, automatic behavior.

Arguably one of the most compelling cues prompting Americans to review their retirement readiness (or, in some cases, stick their heads even deeper into the sand) has come from the state of the economy and the recent financial crisis. Fears around unemployment, changing company retirement and health care benefits, curbed pay increases, and the ever-rising cost of health care have all conspired to provoke more and more people to reconsider what it will take to be able to retire as anticipated.

As Towers Watson discovered in their 2011 Retirement Attitudes survey, the average American worker is acutely aware of their vulnerability when it comes to having enough money to maintain their preretirement lifestyle and the risk of outliving their savings.

The closer they are to the finish line, as is the case with people over 50, the more concerned they are about their retirement security, not just with respect to their own lack of good saving habits, but because of changes being made to existing retirement plan benefits. Almost a quarter of respondents to the Towers Watson survey reported recent changes to their employers' retirement plans, including making the plan unavailable to new hires, freezing benefit increases, or adopting a DB/DC hybrid plan. Additionally, 18 percent cited reduction to or elimination of the employer matching of employee contributions within their 401(k) plan.

The irony is, the Boomer generation (whose concerns about declining retirement account balances and the risks of reduced company retirement benefits are spiking anxiety levels, as reported across many surveys) should never have found themselves in this predicament. Boomers represent the United States' biggest-ever group of earners, collectively earning twice as much ($3.7 trillion) as the "silent" generation that preceded them ($1.6 trillion, according to a

2008 McKinsey & Co. report entitled *Why Baby Boomers Will Need to Work Longer*). But their ratio of debt to net worth is 50 percent higher than the "silents" because Boomers have consumed more and saved less, taking advantage of the availability of easy credit and low interest rates. The topic of consumerism is one we will return to time and again in this book.

Misplaced confidence in the value of their home equity and the belief that returns on their investments were just going to continue going up and up have left (according to the McKinsey report) 69 percent of older Boomers (born 1945–1964) financially ill-prepared for retirement, and many of them don't even realize it. For them, perhaps their best option is to delay the age at which they plan to retire. That, of course, assumes that their skills are still in demand and relevant to the marketplace, or they have the capacity to quickly learn new ones. And that they have the health, vision, hearing, mental and physical agility to remain competitive in today's high-paced (and high-tech) working environments. In some cases there are legal and institutional barriers currently in place that impede people from continuing to work, like airline pilots for example, who are precluded from working beyond a certain age.

Thankfully this isn't the complete picture of life in America today. As we alluded to earlier, there is another group that represents a significant glimmer of hope: those Super Savers or Future Early Retirees who are on target with higher savings levels so that they might experience the later life they have imagined and planned for.

Arguably the clearest picture of how these Future Early Retirees think, feel, and act comes from the TCRS report *A Source of Inspiration: Future Early Retirees* mentioned earlier. So what do we know about these individuals?

We can highlight those characteristics that have helped the Future Early Retirees more successfully realize their retirement readiness goals, but also compare them with the general population captured by the Twelfth Annual Transamerica Center for Retirement Studies Survey which polled U.S. employers and workers on their attitudes toward retirement. From this survey, TCRS found that a full 21 percent of respondents expected to retire before they reached the age of 65. While that might not seem like a large percentage of our population, given the difficulty of just retiring at a normal retirement age, we were encouraged by these statistics. Even more encouraging was that, as previously mentioned, these Future Early Retirees are otherwise not exceptional people. Just over half of them have a college degree, they are mostly in their thirties and forties, and the majority of them earn less than $100,000 a year.

What does make them special, however, is their high degree of confidence that they will be able to retire comfortably and enjoy activities like travel and pursuing hobbies more so than other respondents. Their attitudes and behaviors would lead us to believe this confidence is not misplaced. More than any other group, saving for retirement was cited as their main financial priority. As luminaries since the dawn of humankind have stressed, what we believe and act upon becomes our reality. These Super Savers are certainly evidence of that.

Such optimal savings patterns have led the Future Early Retirees to be more likely to rely on personal savings and investments as an income source in retirement, in addition to 401(k), 403(b), and other workplace retirement accounts. The Future Early Retirees are least likely to expect to rely on Social Security (16 percent versus 30 percent). Unlike the average retiree who expects to give up work at age 65 or later, this early retirement group is relying less on the performance of their investments and hedging their bets with increased savings.

The habits of these Future Early Retirees are worth highlighting. The recession may have hit them just the same as everyone else, but that has not stopped them from saving just as much, if not more, than they did before. They are also better prepared with good habits, including having established a retirement strategy (71 percent of Future Early Retirees compared with 52 percent of Americans generally), having a back-up plan should that strategy not work out (29 percent compared with 16 percent), and being much more personally involved in monitoring and managing their retirement savings accounts (71 percent compared with 58 percent).

They also have more ambitious retirement savings goals: $750,000 compared with $650,000 for those who plan to retire at age 65 and $500,000 for those who plan to retire later. Like Amy Haley, mentioned earlier, the Future Early Retirees are more likely to achieve their goals, given that they defer more of their annual earnings into a company-sponsored plan than other groups.

Nevertheless, these differences aren't all under their own control. The Future Early Retirees are also more likely to have access to a company retirement plan (including pensions, 401(k)s, and similar plans) than those respondents who expect to retire later, making the cooperation of employers with respect to establishing, promoting, and maintaining some form of retirement plan vitally important. The issue of coverage is something we will come back to later in this book.

What is somewhat more complex to get a handle on is the extent to which people want others to make retirement savings decisions for them—as would be the case with "auto-everything" that we discuss in more detail in Chapter 7. For example, while only a small percentage of workers in the Twelfth Annual Transamerica Center for Retirement Studies Survey said that they wanted to hand over this control, the Towers Watson study found that most Americans would in fact prefer others to look after their retirement investments, in exchange for stronger guarantees that their nest egg wouldn't lose its value.

So what is the truth? Many of our industry experts, during our interviews with them, expressed concern about the disengaged nature of many workers when it comes to this vitally important topic of retirement readiness. On several occasions we were told how many of the highly intelligent, professional people that these industry professionals know spend very little time thinking about and preparing for retirement. One example was given where an otherwise well-educated professional, who knew the importance of retirement planning, spent no more than 15 minutes on the topic. And we are not talking about 15 minutes a month here, or even 15 minutes a week, but 15 minutes *a year*. That is considerably less than the time most people typically spend planning a weekend getaway!

So what is causing this aversion to facing up to one's retirement future, at least for the average American?

Perhaps it is the fault of what David Bach termed The Latte Factor®—all that financial advice that says we need to sacrifice our daily latte in order to have better savings levels. But this is not the case for Amy Haley. In fact, because she has intuitively embraced so many of the characteristics of a Future Early Retiree, she is able to enjoy a more balanced life. She told us that there is a cafeteria in the basement of her office building that she visits most days for a breakfast burrito. Okay, that means a few dollars less that she is saving for a rainy day, but since Amy is otherwise doing all the right things she doesn't feel the need to deprive herself. Many of our interviewees echoed that sentiment, pointing out that if you begin early enough and do all the right things you can have both a sufficient retirement nest egg for the future *and* enjoy the present with controlled spending and an occasional splurge.

Which brings us back to our earlier question of just how much is enough when it comes to retirement savings. How do we effectively plan for retirement when we cannot know how long we will live and may significantly outlive our expected longevity; we simply don't know for how many years of retirement we are planning.

As Fred Reish, Partner/Chair of the Fiduciary Services ERISA Team at Drinker Biddle & Reath LLP, pointed out: "I think people would be shocked if they learned that if you retire at age 65 with a $500,000 account balance and you withdraw 5 percent or $25,000 a year, adjusted for inflation each year, that there's a significant risk you could run out of money before you die."

That is where having enough *knowledge* and not just enough *money* to last during retirement comes into play. There has been raging debate in the retirement services industry about the state of financial literacy among plan participants specifically and the average American worker in general. The arguments essentially fall into two camps: one side suggests that we abdicate our long-standing efforts to educate the average American worker on the grounds that financial literacy—even basic financial literacy—is beyond their grasp; the other proclaims that efforts to create informed investors is a moral imperative.

As Todd Lacey, Senior Vice President of Strategic Distribution at Transamerica Retirement Solutions points out, "We've spent a lot of time as an industry trying to educate plan participants on how to invest their retirement accounts. I'm not sure if that's the right approach. Perhaps our mistake as an industry has been putting too much emphasis on creating a lot of doctors when what people really want is just to be cured."

But Lacey goes on to emphasize that while we may not need to create doctors, we do need to ensure the patient (participant) is adequately informed and educated to make fundamentally sound decisions when needed.

As you might imagine, both sides of this argument have merit. While most people will never be truly informed investors, a fundamental understanding of basic financial concepts does seem to be an imperative. Financial literacy is a topic we explore in further detail in Chapter 5.

As previously mentioned, the average current account balance is approximately $60,000, which makes the $500,000 balance Fred mentions a significant accomplishment by most measures. Yet, even with an abnormally high account balance, if improperly managed there is still significant risk of a financial shortfall in retirement. Does the average person understand how to "draw down" their retirement assets? While defined benefit (DB) plans automatically performed this essential draw down of assets by guaranteeing lifetime income, defined contribution (DC) plans like 401(k)s and 403(b)s typically do not. This draw-down feature of a DB plan, often taken for granted by participants, is one of the true gems of the defined benefit plan. DC plans simply present retirees with a balance upon retirement with which they (the retirees) have multiple options. As such, understanding how to make one's income last a lifetime would seem to be essential to achieving security in retirement.

As mentioned earlier, a math problem that has stumped humanity since the beginning of time is trying to calculate our individual life expectancy. While actuarial tables for life expectancy will tell us very precisely how long the average American will live, we simply cannot know how long we, as individuals, will do so. In fact, life expectancy is, by its very definition, the average lifespan of a group of individuals, indicating that approximately half of us will live longer and half of us will not. This concept of outliving our life expectancy—and potentially our income—is known as longevity risk. Arguably one of the more sensible actions people can take is to pool at least a portion of their retirement assets with others. If they do, as a group, their collective lifespan will more closely approximate the average life expectancy. This allows them to more clearly define how long they will (on average) live and create a lifetime stream of income that will help eradicate the anxiety that so many Americans are experiencing these days because they fear that they will run out of money before they die. This concept of lifetime income—and annuities—has recently received a significant amount of attention within the retirement plan industry and will be addressed further, specifically in relation to longevity risk, in Chapter 4. The point we simply want to make here is that there is complexity involved in retirement planning, no less than those issues grappled with by the Clinton Global Initiative, Google's Solve for X, or Eli Lilly's InnoCentive mentioned in the Introduction. As such, an effective long-term solution to retirement readiness will require new and different minds and ideas.

Further, even if we rely heavily on current industry experts to, as Lacey states, "just cure the patient," the average American worker must be equipped with some basic financial knowledge. That would at least prepare them somewhat to navigate the complex decisions surrounding retirement and retirement planning because, at some point in time, they *will* have to make decisions for which they are ultimately solely responsible.

While the Super Savers give us hope, the Ill Prepared dominate our landscape. The Amy Haleys of our world show us the possibilities with discipline, effort, and know-how, perhaps influenced by early childhood relationships like the one Amy had with her grandfather. They have somehow elevated the task of retirement planning to a level of significance in their daily lives. They take the time to enroll in their company retirement plan, to understand their company's benefit structure, and to proactively allocate their accounts to appropriate investments. They set goals and monitor their progress on a regular basis and, as a result, save significantly more for their future. They are somehow able to find a balance between the temptation of rampant consumerism and the pragmatic philosophy espoused by so many retirement plan practitioners: pay yourself first by committing to your future.

Unfortunately, Amy is not the norm . . . not even close. To put it bluntly, the American worker has simply not gotten the memo. Our life expectancies are increasing on a daily basis and the financial burden of retirement goes right along with it. Our appetite for the present still far outweighs our discipline for the future. On the whole, and in stark contrast to the habits of a minority of Super Savers, we don't prioritize saving, we don't take the time to learn and understand our company's benefit structures, and we routinely lose the battle with consumerism. The average American worker has a front row seat on the Titanic, headed for a retirement iceberg.

So whose responsibility is it anyway? As Jay Vivian, who for years ran the IBM retirement fund and describes himself as a Libertarian, realistically pointed out, "Well, it's clearly money to do with as you please. If you decide to blow it all on a long weekend in Las Vegas, or otherwise spend it frivolously, or are unfortunate enough to get robbed of all your savings and possessions—who ends up holding the bag? What we're looking at here—and we are—is a social welfare issue, not just an individual one."

Jay is 100 percent correct: retirement readiness is not just an individual issue and it is not just an industry issue, it is a social issue—and an incredibly important one. There is a lot more at stake here than comfort in retirement. It is really about survival and there is a lot of work that needs to be done to get us back on track.

But let us consider that for a moment. Were we ever on track? By which we mean, was there ever a cohesive vision for retirement embraced by all stakeholders: from individuals to industry, from employers to policymakers?

To answer that question let us take a brief trip back in time to review the history of this concept we call retirement.

Chapter 2

A Brief History of Retirement

Otto von Bismarck would probably increase today's retirement age to 78—or maybe 75, if we give him the benefit of the doubt for mellowing in old age.

—Martin Hüfner, *The Globalist*

Every week, bored and lonely Frank Moses would tear up his Social Security check as a ruse to call and flirt with the woman who processed his government pension. So begins the movie *RED (Retired Extremely Dangerous)*, the 2010 comedy thriller in which four former CIA operatives, including Moses, team up to tote machine guns, break into Langley, evade capture, and expose a scandal involving the Vice President of the United States.

The main characters are played age-appropriately by Bruce Willis, John Malkovich, Helen Mirren, and Morgan Freeman, who average 62 years among them. At one point in the movie Victoria, played by Mirren, admits that she breaks up the monotony of her retired life by taking "the occasional side job."

Contrast that movie with the little-known silent short directed in 1911 by pioneering filmmaker D. W. Griffith (best known for his controversial *The Birth of a Nation*). *What Shall We Do With Our Old?* features an elderly carpenter who becomes one of those workers weeded out by a new foreman in preference for younger, stronger, and more energetic employees. Unable to find new employment because of his age, and with his savings exhausted, the carpenter steals some food for his sick wife and is subsequently arrested.

YouTube viewers can watch the jailing and later release of the old carpenter (to the strains of Tchaikovsky's dramatic *1812 Overture*), after "the kindly judge . . . moved by conscience" sends a policeman to verify his story of having an ailing wife. The group returns with the food to find the woman dead. The final title card declares, "Nothing for the useful citizen wounded in the battle of life," possibly referring to the fact that while Union Army veterans at the time were receiving generous pensions, there was scant financial protection for increasing numbers of older workers whose skills no longer aligned with the needs and pace of modern society.

The early part of the twentieth century offered few, if any, pension provisions outside of the dozen or so private pension plans that were mostly available to employees of public utilities, banks, and large industrial corporations. (The first corporate pension plan in the United States was established by the American Express Company in 1875.) Less than 100 years later marketers were looking for ways to glamorize retirement as a means of helping retirees spend their leisure time—and their money. During that time the concept of retirement has reflected different notions of push and pull between employers and employees.

What is easy to overlook—and what we focus on in this chapter—are the roles that retirement and the emergence of the pension plan have played in our economic, political, and social lives. By reviewing this topic more closely we also want to uncover whether, at any time, there has been a unifying, national vision around retirement.

The Rise of Retirement

For retirement to make any sense at all—the word derives from a sixteenth century verb meaning "to retreat"—there needs to be some period of time between the end of work and the end of one's life. As Mary-Lou Weisman pointed out in her *New York Times* article entitled "The History of Retirement, From Early Man to A.A.R.P.": "In the beginning, there was no retirement. There were no old people."

As our nation transitioned from a largely agricultural society to an industrialized one at the dawn of the twentieth century, the accompanying aging of the workforce presented a challenge. What were we to do with older workers who—whether in reality or otherwise—were perceived as not having the strength, speed, mental agility, and adaptability required by industries that were increasingly influenced by the burgeoning scientific management and efficiency movements? If the United States was to become a global economic powerhouse, its focus needed to be on increased productivity. At the time, retiring older workers in favor of the young made economic sense, given that their longer tenure typically meant they earned higher wages while at the same time their skills sets were no longer as vital as they used to be. As Dora L. Costa writes in *The Evolution of Retirement: An American Economic History 1880–1990*: ". . . the Linotype machine turned the printing industry from a class craft in which type was set by hand in thousands of small shops into an industry that required relatively less skill but greater speed."

In his 1882 science fiction dystopian novel, *The Fixed Period*, English novelist Anthony Trollope (1815–1882) envisioned a futuristic society—the book was set in 1980—in which individuals were forced by law to retire at age 67 and begin a year of contemplation that prepared them to be "peacefully extinguished" by chloroform.

The topic of euthanizing the old became the focus of considerable media attention when Sir William Osler, one of the founders of Johns Hopkins Hospital and its physician-in-chief, delivered his valedictorian address entitled "The Fixed Period" in February 1905.

Reputed to be a practical joker, it is likely that Osler—a mere 55 years old at the time—had his tongue placed firmly in his cheek when he pointed out "the comparative uselessness of men above the age of 40," and "the incalculable benefit it would be in commercial, political, and in professional life if, as a matter of course, men stopped working at the age of 60." This obviously did not apply to him, given that Osler subsequently accepted a post at Oxford University, where he worked until he died at 70.

It wasn't just slower factory hands that faced the age discrimination that began to rear its ugly head as the working population began to age. Decades before Arthur Miller wrote *Death of a Salesman* (1949)—in which the low productivity of the main character, 60-year-old Willy Loman, rendered him a liability to the company—salesmen in late middle age and beyond were resorting to dying their hair, among other things, in an effort to look more youthful. Magazines like

Salesmanship ("Devoted to Success in Selling") were promoting the new professionalism of their business, for which older salesmen were thought not well suited.

According to William Graebner, author of *A History of Retirement: The Meaning and Function of an American Institution 1885–1978*: "A 65-year-old salesman named Elder confronted reality rather than theory when the assistant director of sales and the vice president requested his retirement under the company's new pension plan because he was 'too old a man to adopt our present methods' and because he was not sufficiently active to adequately cover his large territory."

Elder was, nevertheless, one of the lucky ones, given that his company did at least offer employees a pension plan. Private defined benefit plans (meaning that contributions were made solely by the employer, not by employees, and the benefit was defined at retirement in the form of a stable income stream) were still relatively rare.

The popularity of the private pension plan began to grow following changes in the tax system that, beginning in 1916, allowed sums furnished by a corporation to a fiduciary-managed employee pension trust—thereby keeping them completely separate from company assets—to be deductible from gross corporate income.

Extending the nineteenth century sensibility of paternalism toward one's employees, the economic benefits of attracting workers by offering a defined benefit pension plan became apparent. For example, in a note to chemical manufacturer Thomas Coleman du Pont, cited by Graebner, retired banker George W. Perkins wrote: "I have never heard of any plan except one that would assist in regulating salaries and that is a pension plan. . . . The right sort of pension plan comes pretty near being a panacea for most of the ills that exist between employer and employee."

In many respects Perkins was right. Knowing they had a pension to fall back on gave aging employees in the first few decades of the twentieth century a sense of security, impacting their state of mind and, as a consequence, their productivity. And, from the employer's perspective, the pension helped reduce turnover and mitigate the demand for higher wages.

In economic terms, then, these early pension plans served a variety of purposes: They were a form of permanent unemployment relief for older workers who were unable to get jobs; they helped open up jobs for younger workers and incentivized them with the promise of promotions; and they deferred wage increases with the promise of security in retirement.

Unfortunately, the early days of the defined benefit plan being characterized as the "good old days" is largely a myth and so the issue of old-age dependency remained. As Graebner points out, by 1932 only 15 percent of Americans were covered by such plans, with "perhaps 5 percent of those who needed benefits . . . actually receiving them." The rules under which employees qualified for payments tended to be onerous. For example, few plans provided benefits for workers' spouses, they often required a minimum of 15 years of service, and "only 10 percent of the plans legally obligated the company to any kind of payment. Additionally, because few of the plans were contributory, most did not offer the advantages of accumulated forced savings."

So, as the twentieth century marched on it became clear that something had to be done at the federal level to protect U.S. citizens from the harsh realities of modern life. A number of states had tried but not always succeeded in instituting old-age pension plans, such as Massachusetts in 1903, Arizona in 1915, and Pennsylvania in 1923. What really turned this into a major political issue was the Great Depression, which began in 1929 and lasted approximately 10 years.

Long periods of unemployment during that time wiped out people's savings. Those workers who relied on private or trade union pension plans for their security found that most of them had been discontinued or their benefits slashed. Public sympathy for the elderly, especially now that even the middle class risked ending up in almshouses, had swelled to such proportions that politicians were compelled to look for ways to institute some form of assistance at the federal level. For inspiration, they turned to nineteenth century Germany and the brainchild of that country's Iron Chancellor.

Politics and the Pension

The distinction for having helped to create the world's first national social insurance system goes to German Chancellor Otto von Bismarck (1815–1898). Recognizing the rising appeal of Marxism in his country, he was determined to counter their demands for increasingly extreme measures with a "socialist" plan of his own. Persuading William the First that social welfare of the poor was an issue of national survival at a time of increasing volatility, the Emperor wrote to the German Parliament in 1881, "Those who are disabled from work by age and invalidity have a well-grounded claim to care from the state."

Bismarck is frequently yet wrongly credited with having influenced the United States to set the demarcation line for old age at 65 years—the point at which most people are considered pensionable. As the Social Security Administration's website points out, Bismarck had nothing at all to do with it.

The age at which Germans were eligible to receive old age and disability insurance was originally set in 1889 at 70 years, not 65. Given that very few people lived that long in those days (Bismarck himself was a notable exception, being 74 at the time), this was not planned to be an expensive program. That age limit was shifted down to 65 in 1916, at which point Bismarck had been dead for 18 years. While in many other parts of Europe and the world (as in Germany) 65 remains the official retirement age, the United States has taken steps to delay Social Security payments as a result of our living much longer than we did at the dawn of the twentieth century. Whereas life expectancies have increased significantly, however, the Social Security retirement age has only increased by two years, from 65 to 67.

Why did the United States originally decide upon 65 as the retirement age when the Committee on Economic Security (CES) was drafting its recommendations for Social Security Old Age Insurance, enacted in 1935 as part of President Franklin Delano Roosevelt's New Deal?

According to Social Security Online, the decision was influenced by the fact that while the private and state old-age pension systems in force at that time were equally split between setting the retirement age at 65 and age 70, the new federal Railroad Retirement System, passed by Congress in 1934, leaned toward 65 as the age for workers to retire. Actuarial studies used at the time sealed the deal.

Social Security Old Age Insurance was, like the Union Army pension provisions, originally limited in scope—but that soon changed. According to Costa, only 43 percent of the labor force was covered when the law went into effect, since workers on the railroads, in agriculture, domestic workers, and the self-employed were excluded. Government workers also did not qualify, but were separately covered under a law enacted in 1920.

The American Social Security system mirrored Bismarck's German model in that contributions were required from employees, employers, *and* the government in order to avoid future costs becoming overwhelming, according to the Committee on Economic Security.

As originally conceived, a worker who died before they reached the age of 65 could receive a money-back guarantee from Social Security, equal to his individual contributions plus interest. Benefit payments were to be deferred until 1942, by which time a significant surplus was expected to have accrued from increases in the payroll tax rate. This rate was to increase incrementally from 2 percent on the first $3,000 earnings during the years 1937 to 1939, with yearly increases thereafter of 1 percent until that figure reached 6 percent in 1949, at which point it was presumably to be capped.

The thinking was that as payroll taxes were being paid and accumulating, the earned interest and revenues that had accrued by 1949 "would support the system indefinitely."

Countering arguments that increasing demands on the system could be met by borrowing from future beneficiaries in order to make payments to present ones, the Secretary of the Treasury Henry Morgenthau stated that placing confidence in the taxing power of the future to meet current needs was a perspective he did not share, saying "We cannot safely expect future generations to continue to divert such large sums to the support of the aged unless we lighten the burden upon the future in other directions. . . . We desire to establish this system on such sound foundations that it can be continued indefinitely in the future" (Costa 1998, 173).

Unfortunately the population trends that Roosevelt's Committee on Economic Security used to predict that by 1990 more than 12 percent of the American populace would be over 64 years of age did not foresee the postwar baby boom, which ended up rendering their modest provisions insufficient.

Also unfortunate was the fact that Morgenthau's actuarial principles were abandoned because of intense political pressure, including concern in some quarters that the unspent surplus could be raided by government spending. Amendments to the Social Security Act in 1939 removed the money-back guarantee, payouts were set to begin in 1940 not 1942, and the 1 percent increase in payroll taxes that was due to begin that same year was repealed.

While a fascinating topic in and of itself, not least because of the current challenges we are facing and concerns about the future viability of Social Security in the twenty-first century, readers interested in further exploration are recommended to look to the books already mentioned, by Graebner and Costa.

But just because the environment was set up for workers to retire at age 65 with *some* financial provisions put in place, it didn't necessarily mean that the average American at the time was quick to adapt to the relatively new concept of an extended, leisured retirement. For many the notions of transitioning from a producer to a consumer and facing a span of retirement that more than doubled that of the previous generation were so alien that that chairman of a conference sponsored by glass manufacturer Corning in May 1951 suggested, "Perhaps we have to glamorize leisure as we have not."

Marketing the Senior Citizen

When we think of those people we know who fall under the collective term "the retired," we are unlikely to recognize the description offered by Irish poet W. B. Yeats (1865–1939) who, in *When You Are Old,* refers to being "gray and full of sleep and nodding by the fire." Even Eleanor Roosevelt referenced a similarly sedentary image of retirement when she reminded the audience listening to her talk entitled "Old Age Pensions" the year before her husband passed the Social Security Act that "Old people love their own things even more than young people do. It means so much to sit in the same old chair you sat in for a great many years, to see the same picture that you always looked at!"

Less than two decades later, when society's focus had well and truly shifted from producing goods to stimulating consumerism, who better than the retired to populate this new frontier of leisure and spending? Indeed, by the 1950s, the lives of the over-60s were starting to be completely transformed.

As workforce participation rates declined and the average health of the elderly improved, mid-twentieth century retirees could expect considerably more golden years than had been anticipated in

Bismarck's day. Plus, they now had plenty more outlets for their increased wealth: the availability of mass tourism; the popularity of Arizona, California, and Florida as places with better weather and communities designed for the elderly; the rapidly booming entertainment industry; and cheaper sporting and recreational goods.

But getting people to take advantage of these opportunities required a change of focus. So began the marketing of life as a senior citizen. Even the word retirement came under scrutiny. In their first issue of *Retirement Planning News*, the editors took umbrage with the concept of the "withdrawal from the active world" that the term implied and suggested renaming this life stage "the fulfillment years," a time when the retiree had the "opportunity to fulfill lifelong desires to do things he never quite had time to do before."

Many large insurance companies, in which men were now required to retire at 65 and women at age 60, created formal retirement preparation programs to assist them. Some of the larger American companies even went as far as to introduce messaging about retirement to employees who had reached the age of 50, the idea being that happiness during retirement wasn't a given—it had to be planned for.

For example, in his admonition that "the best of life is yet to come," the Vice President of Mutual Life Insurance addressed a 1952 meeting of the National Industrial Conference Board by stressing the need to sell retirement "by constant stories of happily retired people telling what they do, but still more, of course, emphasizing what they did to get ready for the life they are now living" (Freedman 2007, 46).

In some camps, at least, it was not just a question of simply preparing people psychologically for retirement. Joy Elmer Morgan, editor of *Senior Citizen*, used this platform to remind readers that maturity, responsibility, and self-discipline were the hallmarks of those who called themselves senior citizens, adding that: "Failure to face the later years and to plan for them is a sign of infantilism and immaturity."

Ironically, whereas as a society we soon enthusiastically embraced the concept of retirement, we seem—in large part—to have misplaced that mid-twentieth century sense of personal responsibility of planning for comfortable and stress-free fulfillment years.

Where Is the Vision?

That is a broad outline of how we got to where we are today.

Not surprisingly, over the past century the concepts of the pension plan and retirement have morphed in relation to prevailing social, economic, and political pressures. In its earliest stages, the concept of retirement was seen economically as helping to replace less productive aging workers with younger ones; to maintain loyalty among valued employees and defer wage increases; and to provide a level of security that paternalistic employers felt was their responsibility toward their employees. How are we to view it today? Simply stated, we feel it is the right thing to do to ensure that every American who wants or needs to can retire with dignity and in some degree of comfort.

The challenge that lies before us is the fact that while our longevity has increased substantially—in that we are now living many more years than our early twentieth century forebears—the retirement age has not shifted. While there are a lot of conversations going on around this topic among the various stakeholders—not least employers, industry professionals, policymakers, and the media—we have not yet succeeded in viewing this issue systemically, uniting around a single, coherent, compelling vision.

As we discussed earlier, the average American worker has fallen woefully behind in the battle for a fully funded retirement. As the bulk of the Boomers rapidly approach retirement with an average 401(k) account balance of just $60,000 (across all ages) and very few years left to save, for many the definition of retirement has to change once again.

While the message we deliver to those who have not saved enough and still plan to retire at age 65 may have to be, "You simply can't," it is incumbent upon all of us to change that reality for the next generation and those who follow.

In a moment of honest reflection, we need to ask ourselves: is what we are doing today going to produce better results for Generation X (born between 1965 and 1979) and the Millennials (born after 1979), or are we on a hamster wheel destined for a similar unsuccessful outcome in perpetuity?

The good news is that there seems to be a genuine groundswell of belief that the battle for retirement readiness is at an inflection point in the United States and that as our society witnesses the Boomers slide into retirement largely unprepared, more and more people will embrace this challenge and help us change the outcome.

But, as Dr. Seuss once wrote, "Should you turn left or right . . . or right-and-three-quarters? Or, maybe, not quite?" Without a clear vision to lead us forward, the challenge may prove to be too large and a successful outcome too far out of reach. So where do we find inspiration for a vision worthy of a challenge this important? Our history is rich with examples of bold visions on tough issues that have led to successful outcomes. And in the next chapter we turn to, arguably, one of the most famous bold visions in recent history.

Chapter 3

State of the Union

Houston, we have a problem.

—*Apollo 13* (movie)

"I believe that this nation should commit itself to achieving the goal, before this decade is out, of landing a man on the Moon and returning him safely to the Earth."

Those words were spoken by John F. Kennedy, before a joint session of Congress on May 25, 1961, as he outlined his vision for the United States space program.

As he finished laying out his four-part plan for space exploration, President Kennedy went on to state, ". . . let it be clear that I am asking the Congress and the country to accept a firm commitment to a new course of action, a course which will last for many years and carry very heavy costs: $531 million in fiscal '62—an estimated $7 to $9 billion additional over the next five years. If we are to go only half way, or reduce our sights in the face of difficulty, in my judgment it would be better not to go at all."

It just can't get any clearer than that statement of purpose. Not surprisingly, the ensuing decade proved to be one of the most productive eras of space exploration in United States history. Yet while the challenge was clear and the gauntlet thrown down, our resolve was to be tested on many occasions.

Some nine years later, on April 11, 1970, Apollo 13 launched from Kennedy Space Center at Cape Canaveral, Florida. On board were Commander James A. Lovell, Command Module Pilot John L. "Jack"

Swigert, and Lunar Module Pilot Fred W. Haise. Apollo 13's mission was to explore the Fra Mauro Formation on the Moon, and a successful landing would make these the third set of Apollo astronauts to reach the lunar surface since JFK's declaration in 1961. They would never make it, but JFK's vision would once again be tested and would hold true.

Two days after liftoff an oxygen tank exploded onboard the spacecraft and the lunar landing had to be aborted. The world spent the next three days on edge, watching with trepidation as the laser-focused crew and entire support staff doggedly tackled the myriad of challenges and brought the crippled lunar module and crew safely back to Earth. In all, they were in space for 5 days, 22 hours, 54 minutes, and 41 seconds. The highly celebrated touchdown occurred in the South Pacific Ocean on April 17, 1970.

In one poignant scene in Ron Howard's movie *Apollo 13*, the director of NASA is being briefed on the many challenges facing the module as it prepares for reentry into the Earth's atmosphere: from the angle of its trajectory to warnings about a typhoon close to the recovery area. Having considered everything that could go wrong, the director comments that ". . . this could be the worst disaster NASA's ever experienced." At which point Flight Commander Kranz (played by Ed Harris) responds: "With all due respect, sir, I believe this is gonna be our finest hour." As we know, he was proven right.

John F. Kennedy once said, "When written in Chinese, the word 'crisis' is composed of two characters. One represents danger and the other represents opportunity." The Apollo 13 story depicts NASA (and a nation) facing the possibility of its greatest disaster, yet through sheer determination, teamwork, and a clear vision, opportunity emerges. NASA's finest hour is only possible in contrast to the devastating result that could have been. It's a wonderful reminder for us all to let the story play out, rather than prejudging its outcome.

As discussed previously, we are indeed in the throes of a retirement-readiness crisis and the challenge is of epic proportions. We have to remind ourselves that the play is not yet over, the story has not yet been written, and that ultimately it's our responsibility to get the ending right. Perhaps our finest hour is yet to come.

There is arguably no better example of teamwork, determination, and clarity of focus than the rescue of Apollo 13. The vision was abundantly clear: to get the astronauts back home safely to Earth. Every member of the team understood this and applied the full weight of their efforts to accomplishing the task at hand. Without this clarity, would the results have been the same? Likely not. Well then, if clarity of focus is so important to an outcome, we have to ask ourselves . . . how clear is our focus on providing retirement readiness? Do we have an overarching mission and is the team galvanized around it? What is our vision for the American worker in retirement and, if it is clear, how committed are we to it?

While saving Apollo 13 will never be characterized as an easy task, the definition of success was actually quite simple: bring three astronauts safely back to Earth . . . full stop. In comparison, defining a successful outcome surrounding the retirement readiness effort is significantly more complex.

Personalizing Success

While we have well-developed theories about the amount of assets that need to be accumulated, income replacement ratios, sustainable withdrawal rates, and an abundance of sophisticated tools to help us calculate the lot of them, retirement readiness will always be based on the individual's needs and preferences . . . and, boy, is that messy. One size will never fit all.

Let's take, for instance, the concept of an 80 percent income replacement ratio, which is often used as the standard for how much of one's working income needs to be replaced in retirement. In reality, that replacement ratio is going to vary dramatically depending on many factors, not the least of which is lifestyle in retirement. This was reinforced many times in our interviews, but never more clearly than in our discussion with Paul Henry of LIMRA, an organization which "provides research, consulting, and other services to insurance and financial services companies, worldwide."

"One of the things we've tried to do with our 'Ready to Retire' application is to get people to visualize not an abstract retirement, but a very personal retirement and one that incorporates things that are meaningful to them today. And what we've seen is that when people do that there's sort of this light bulb that goes on; there's this aha moment and all of a sudden they realize that they have a potential problem."

There simply is no single definition of success as it relates to retirement readiness, and that makes it a challenge. But let's revisit JFK's overall vision for the space program in 1961: It too was complex and required a single focus to ensure its success.

The Hallmark of a Civilized Society

In our quest to better understand what might constitute a common vision around retirement readiness, we asked our interviewees the question: what defines a civilized society as it relates to financial security in retirement? Here are just a few of the many responses we received, the first being one we already showcased in the Introduction:

Charlie Ruffel: "At the end of the day, the basic premise here that what fundamentally defines a civilized society is, after decades of work, being able to retire with financial dignity. That is an absolute hallmark of a civilized society."

Paul D'Aiutolo: "I believe it's continuity of quality of life. Society has an obligation to ensure that, with their hard work, people have an opportunity to maintain their quality of life in retirement. We don't have an obligation to make their lifestyle better, just to preserve it when they can no longer work."

Chad Larsen: "Certainly a central component of what retirement means in a civilized society is that you don't have some people in abject poverty and wondering where the next meal is coming from and another segment of your society that is not only living in luxury but indifferent to those who are suffering."

Dallas Salisbury: "A civilized society, when it comes to old age, is the ability of individuals to spend their later years with dignity and a sufficient level of comfort to be happy that they are alive. That doesn't mean replacement of preretirement lifestyle, frankly. It does mean a roof over your head and decent food on the table and some decent health care, and hopefully the ability to have some family around."

The similarity of these responses is striking. None of our interviewees believed that a civilized society owed anyone a life of travel, of hobbies, or luxuries of any kind, unlike the marketing messages aimed at making retirement more palatable to Americans in the 1950s. For our interviewees, the concept of wealth didn't come up, even once, perhaps as a result of how the question was phrased. There were certain recurring themes that characterized virtually every response we heard. The concept of "financial dignity" was the most commonly recurring, with "maintaining ones current lifestyle" a close second. Terms like "comfort," "sufficient," and "quality of life" were often cited. And while the terms "our obligation" and "our responsibility" came up often in relation to ensuring everyone had a fair opportunity, they were almost always used conditionally, and dependent on the recipient having worked hard and made a diligent effort to save. The theme of hard work came up over and over, with a clear message that retirement was an earned right, rather than an absolute one.

It was interesting to see that what was completely missing from the discussion was the expectation that a worker's retirement should be dependent on their having made intelligent investment decisions. There seemed to be a general acknowledgement that being investment savvy should not determine one's ability to retire. In all, the central message seemed to be that we believe anyone who works hard and makes a sincere effort deserves financial dignity in retirement.

If, in the end, a common vision among retirement industry professionals is to provide financial security for the average American worker who has spent a lifetime working hard, collecting a paycheck, and living within his or her means, are we—the team—truly staying focused on those tasks that will move us closer to this end? What does our Command Center look like? Are we focused on mission-critical tasks, or do we tend to get distracted by those things that simply don't move the needle and won't get us closer to dignity in retirement for those who want and need it?

The Current Command Center

Let's look at the state of the union, by which we mean the team of professionals who currently work in the qualified retirement plan space, and review their current focus.

The qualified retirement plan industry is a highly technical field with complicated tax rules, more than its share of compliance requirements, and a great deal of perceived liability for its many stakeholders. At its core, it represents an intersection of the Internal Revenue Code, as amended, the Employee Retirement Income Security Act (ERISA), as well as related legislation and regulations. It's also a blend of investments, employee communications, and human behavior. So who are these stakeholders and what is their respective involvement in bringing retirement plans to the American worker?

Every qualified retirement plan—meaning either a defined benefit or defined contribution plan that is qualified under the Internal Revenue Code—starts with a plan document, which essentially governs the operation of the plan itself. This plan document needs to be carefully drafted to comply with the Internal Revenue Code rules and regulations governing qualified retirement plans and to fit the needs of the company for which it is being designed. The plan document must then be maintained, amending and restating it as required by updates to legislation, new regulations, and any changes to plan design, to ensure it continues to meet the needs of the company sponsoring the plan. This work is typically done by an ERISA attorney, a third-party administrator (TPA), or a bundled-plan provider (recordkeeper)—or all three working in conjunction—and is incredibly important to the outcome of the participant, since it essentially sets forth the rules of the plan (within the confines of permissibility). As such, the creator has the ability to establish the context of the plan and create powerful contextual factors that can drive participant behavior.

Further, company-sponsored retirement plans, like 401(k) or 403(b) plans, are complicated and need to provide services far beyond those required by a standalone investment account. An individual investment account serves only one investor, is typically offered by a broker-dealer or mutual fund company, often offers a virtually unlimited array of investment choices, and follows a suitability standard of care, which essentially means the investments held by an individual have to be suitable to that individual's circumstances. In contrast, company-sponsored retirement plans have an additional layer of complexity. First of all, they are held to a fiduciary standard of care under ERISA. As such, company-sponsored plans are required to have a named fiduciary (which is typically the plan sponsor or employer) that has visibility into the plan, its assets, and all of its participants and is required to act solely in their best interests. This, along with other requirements for visibility into assets, annual participant deposits, participants' annual income levels, as well as requirements to communicate with and educate employees on plan participation, places a significantly higher recordkeeping burden on company-sponsored plans.

Recordkeepers (also referred to as plan providers) play the very important role of managing plan data, providing employee and plan communications, and providing the infrastructure needed to manage a qualified retirement plan so that the plan fiduciary can fulfill his/her duties.

Since recordkeepers/plan providers often provide communications to plan participants, they have the ability to shape the message that participants will ultimately hear. As such, they have often been relied on to help drive participation for plan sponsors, advisors, and TPAs by offering onsite employee education, automatic enrollment programs, web education, employee communication, and much more.

All retirement plans, corporate or otherwise, must have investments in which to invest plan assets (typically consisting of participant and company contributions). Most company-sponsored retirement plans offer a variety of managed investment products as their core plan investments such as: stable value funds, mutual funds, collective investment trusts, and sub-advised separate accounts. Typically, the role of providing the investment expertise to plans is the role of the investment provider. Often, plans will have many mutual funds or separate accounts, representing varying investment styles, from multiple investment companies (often mutual fund providers).

Although these investment providers may not have direct contact with the participant and often don't even have direct contact with the plan, they do have the ability to influence participant behavior. Many investment providers actively develop participant communication materials that can be used by the recordkeeper or plan sponsor to encourage participants to join the plan, diversify their investments, or even increase contributions.

As previously mentioned, corporate retirement plans have a fairly significant compliance, testing, and administrative burden. In many cases, this burden is shared by the named plan administrator (usually the company sponsoring the plan), which is also referred to as the plan sponsor and an outside administrator, typically referred to as a third-party administrator (TPA). The company is typically responsible for interacting with employees, maintaining and providing payroll records, and ensuring the plan is offered to employees when they become eligible. The TPA is responsible for the technical aspects of managing the plan, like the tax filings, compliance testing, designing and maintaining documents, to name just a few. Both can have significant influence on participant behavior.

TPAs are often considered the technical experts for the plan, certainly as it relates to matters such as plan compliance, testing, and design. As such, they often have the ear of the plan sponsor and can have significant influence on plan design (both initially and ongoing) and plan operation. As previously mentioned, plan design, because it establishes contextual factors that can drive participation, such as automatically enrolling a participant, can dramatically influence participant behavior. Plan sponsors, because of their close connection to the participant, could be one of the most powerful participant influencers, but typically they are not because of their inclination to remain neutral and let employees make an unencumbered decision.

Advisors and Lawyers

So how does the plan sponsor navigate the complexities of hiring a recordkeeper, TPA, and investment provider when they may have very little expertise in the field of retirement? Once they have selected a provider, how do they choose and maintain the underlying investments for their particular plan? Who helps to guide their participants in selecting the investments for their accounts? This is typically where the retirement plan advisor steps in. Although the role of the retirement plan advisor varies dramatically according to their own value proposition and their choice of the aforementioned service providers they work with, they often serve as the lead role for the team servicing the plan. As such, they can and often do play a profound role in participant behavior.

As previously mentioned, qualified retirement plans are highly regulated and where regulations exist, so does liability, and there is often the need for clear interpretation of both. Although there are several bodies of law that are relevant to the retirement plan industry, such as securities and tax law, ERISA is the primary body of law that governs qualified retirement plans. As such, ERISA lawyers play a significant role in helping to navigate the maze of liability, current and pending legislation, and helping the industry mold current interpretation to better serve participants. Many of the newest tools, like automatic enrollment, automatic escalation, and qualified default investment alternatives (QDIAs—to be discussed in more detail in a future chapter) are a direct result of recent legislation and subsequent interpretation by ERISA lawyers.

Throughout the preceding paragraphs, we have made reference to regulation, legislation, compliance, and oversight. Employer retirement plans and policies dictating their role relative to government benefits and other savings vehicles are ultimately determined by policymakers, and specifically through federal legislation. However, retirement plans are regulated through a combination of law, tax code, and rules from various federal government agencies. While many different facets of government are involved in qualified retirement plans, most prevalent are: Congress for enacting new pension legislation, the Internal Revenue Service (IRS) for tax qualification, and the Department of Labor (DOL) for enforcement and participant protection. Since policymakers essentially set and enforce the rules by which the entire industry has to operate, they clearly have powerful influence over participant behavior.

While there are many other parties that serve various parts of the retirement plan industry, the preceding list is meant to broadly outline the primary stakeholders that routinely interact, either directly or indirectly, with plan participants and plan sponsors. In addition to the aforementioned, there are passionately dedicated research and industry organizations that typically operate as nonprofits and do a tremendous amount of good for the industry. A significant number of our interviewees come from such organizations. There are many organizations that provide services, such as educational materials, expertise, and technical support to the entire industry. Finally, there are think tanks, trade organizations, and events that serve to keep the industry well informed. It's a large and complex industry with many moving parts.

If that is our Command Center staff, are we focused on mission-critical tasks? Or are we getting distracted?

We caught up with Fred Reish, a prominent ERISA attorney and a true participant advocate, to ask him whether as an industry we tend to get distracted by those things that ultimately do not improve retirement readiness. We wanted to know whether, in a world of finite resources, we should be focused on those things that really drive results, like getting employees to participate, driving up their contribution rates, and increasing financial literacy, instead of being so hyperfocused on investment monitoring and perceived employer liability? Did he think we could stay focused on these important topics?

This was his response:

Not perfectly, but generally. I think there's an old saying that the wheels of justice grind slowly but exceedingly fine. And another thing about the stock market is that in the short run it's a voting machine; in the long run it's a weighing machine. What I mean is that in the short run there are going to be all kinds of issues that we focus on, but later on, we'll look back at them and decide that our time wasn't well spent.

Early on, plan sponsors were afraid they were going to get sued if they offered fiduciary advice to participants. If you go back 10 years or so, that was a big issue, but it never happened. So we do tend to head off on tangents; but over a period of time we're getting it right. We sometimes deal with problems in the wrong order. For example, in hindsight we should have been using target date funds 20 years ago but we didn't get to them until 10 years after that.

So we don't always deal with things in the right order and we sometimes get distracted from time to time but with a long enough time horizon we get it right. Now why? Why do we get it right with a long enough time horizon? Because in the final analysis, it's all about the participant.

The short-run distractions are where we tend to make the issues about us, about the providers, about the advisors, about the lawyers, about the broker-dealers or whoever. But then we refocus, because the system ultimately is about the participant and you can only deny that reality for so long. We come back to due north, and due north is how real people retire in a reasonable way on their 401(k) plans and Social Security.

That should be our compass, our lighthouse. We're always going to get distracted. But, I don't think we get away from it for too long or that we get away from it in too bad a way.

Fred is right . . . on all counts.

We in the retirement services industry can get distracted in the short run, but in the longer run we are moving in the right direction. That said, few would argue against our need to accelerate our progress. But how might we do that? We have to recognize that in a world of finite resources and one where there is a need for immediate results, any deviation from due north burns valuable fuel.

During our interviews, we were struck by the quality of thought leadership shared by our interviewees, but perhaps equally important we were struck by the palpable passion we felt . . . in every interview. Our conclusion was that the lacking state of retirement readiness has little to do with the commitment and passion of people within the industry known as the "401(k) Whisperers," a dedicated group of practitioners who figuratively (if not literally) lay awake at night trying to solve for that master key needed to unlock the problem of achieving retirement readiness for all—people whom we reference throughout this book.

Further, our interviewees underscore the fact that this issue of retirement readiness is not a retirement industry issue at all, but rather a complicated social issue that needs broad social involvement to make real progress. Yet somehow it seems as though the heavy lifting is being left up to the retirement industry to figure it out, as in "figure out new ways to communicate and to change the context to make it easier to participate in retirement plans." Put simply, the retirement services industry cannot do this alone.

What is really needed is a vision for retirement readiness that is brand agnostic to service provider, policymaker, and plan sponsor. A vision that is focused on the participant and takes into account those aspects we all seem to agree on—in short that anyone who works hard and makes a sincere effort deserves financial dignity in retirement. Wouldn't that be a pretty good place to start for our cohesive vision?

Perhaps. But before we make that decision, let us hold that thought while we take a look at how the modern pension system has evolved over time and where it currently stands today.

Chapter 4

Rise of the DC Plan

The private retirement system was horrible. It was wretched.
—Ted Benna, "Father of the 401(k)"

Cast your mind back to when you scheduled an appointment, thinking you had allowed plenty of time to get there from an earlier commitment on the other side of town. Your car was filled with gas, it had recently been serviced and, despite the fact that you had made the same trip several times, to be on the safe side you printed out the directions and preprogrammed your GPS. What, then, were your chances of arriving at your destination at exactly the right time, using the route you had used on previous occasions? The odds were a lot lower than you might have imagined.

Whether we like to think of it this way or not (and, as Nassim Nicholas Taleb argues in his book *The Black Swan,* the human default is not), life is more about probabilities than guaranteed outcomes. Fooling ourselves that we are always in control often ends up embarrassing us when unexpected delays shred our business schedules. As Sir Frances Bacon identified more than 400 years ago, life is a lot more volatile, chaotic—and considerably less orderly—than we are prone to believe it to be. And thinking that we can accurately know what is going to happen in advance of it being so has caused no end of difficulties when applied to the management of defined benefit (DB) pension plans.

In this chapter we are going to explore why it is that DB plans have become a significant liability to companies, especially larger ones, and

43

why many have moved their organizations away from DB plans in favor of defined contribution (DC) plans. Much like our hypothetical business appointment analogy, despite the best of intentions, the promise of a DB pension plan as a means of ensuring a comfortable retirement has become increasingly difficult for companies to keep. We will also explore whether defined benefits were ever really ubiquitous for the American worker and if the retirement paternalism of the past was a reality. Finally, we will examine the evolution of DC plans as the pendulum has swung from simplicity to complexity and is now swinging back toward simplicity again.

Before doing so, here's a small disclaimer. What we are offering is not meant to be a comprehensive or particularly detailed coverage of these topics. While those who have considerably more knowledge of the evolution of pension plans in the United States may raise an eyebrow (or worse) at our simplification of this issue, the purpose of this chapter is simply to highlight why DC plans overtook DB plans in popularity and to bring attention to many of the challenges around retirement readiness that the average American worker faces as a result.

Defined Benefit Plans

In recent years, there has been a tremendous amount of discussion about defined benefit pension plans in both the private and public sectors. The spotlight has been frequently on the issue of underfunded plans—this relates to a plan's ability to meet its payment obligations to employees and retirees—with the focus of such discussions often resting on the auto giants, airlines, and state and local government pension funds. Occasionally, the conversation shifts from the *possibility* of a pension failure to a real-life example.

One of the most significant pension failures that resulted in over 4,000 U.S. workers receiving little or no pension benefits was that of Studebaker, the automobile manufacturing company that closed its doors in 1963 and terminated its employee pension plan.

Studebaker's collapse placed a spotlight on the vulnerability of all workers with respect to pension rights and recourse, and highlighted a need for regulation and accountability. As a result, landmark legislation—ERISA—was enacted in 1974 by President Gerald Ford who said, "Under this law the men and women of our labor force will have much more clearly defined rights to pension funds and greater assurances that retirement dollars will be there when they are needed."

Part of what ERISA accomplished was to regulate the vesting and participation requirements of pension plans, eliminating any ambiguity as to who was eligible for benefits. As long as an employee met prestated minimum age and service requirements, they would receive a pension under their company's plan. In addition, ERISA established the Pension Benefit Guaranty Corporation (PBGC), a governmental body set up to "protect the retirement incomes of more than 44 million American workers in more than 27,500 private-sector defined benefit pension plans." Despite ERISA's protective qualities, DB plans still depended on their underlying investments to help keep them funded.

So what happens today when a company files for bankruptcy or can no longer meet its pension obligations?

As an employee or retiree of a company in this predicament, you would receive a formal letter concerning the determination of your pension benefit from the PBGC. The letter would indicate that the PBGC would continue paying out benefits to you, as well as be responsible for payments for those yet to retire. That is the good news. The bad news is that, under federal regulations, the yearly maximum benefit a 65-year-old retiree can receive from the PBGC currently stands at just under $56,000. This is unlikely to be a reassuring sum to those long-standing employees earning a higher-than-average salary, since it is often significantly less than they would otherwise have received.

The PBGC is charged with effectively taking over pension funds that fail. It meets these obligations by accumulating premiums that Congress determines must be paid by sponsors of DB plans so that should a company go bankrupt, a certain portion of employees' pensions would be guaranteed. As of this writing, according to their website, the PBGC pays monthly retirement benefits to almost 744,000 retirees who had originally been participants in one of 4,000 pension plans that went under. While the solvency of the PBGC is not a topic we intend to cover, we would be remiss in failing to acknowledge the significant stress on the PBGC as a result of past pension failures and those likely to happen in the future.

How Underfunding Happens

On their surface, DB plans seem to be quite simple. They are essentially a promise made by a plan to its participants to continue to pay a fixed monthly amount in retirement. Why, then, is there so much discussion about underfunded pension plans? To understand the problem, we need to look beyond the simplistic accusations of wrongdoing and examine the risks and complexities inherent in maintaining a DB plan, which serves to explain why we have seen the shift to the DC alternative.

Essentially, the companies that sponsor DB plans are the ones that fund them. Their pension liabilities refer to the estimated cost of paying out benefits to all participants in the plan, and pension assets refer to the money in the plan that will be used to pay those liabilities. The concept of a fully funded plan is pretty simple: assets are equal to liabilities. If assets are lower than liabilities, the plan is termed underfunded, and in those rare circumstances where assets are greater than liabilities, the plan is overfunded.

So what is complicated about all of this? Well, consider this: since the DB plan promises to pay out an income for a participant's entire lifetime or essentially defines the benefit at some future date, all of the risk for making that happen in the future belongs to the plan sponsor. We are right back to our appointment analogy. Similar to the way that we can never predict exactly when and how we will make it across town, we can never know how all the variables will work out when funding a DB plan.

Now let us examine the liability side of the equation and what factors increase a plan's liability, Since most pension formulas rely on length of service and salary (in some form) to set the actual benefit, the longer that employees are tenured and the higher their salaries, the greater the increase in pension liabilities. But the real culprit here is longevity. The longer retirees live in retirement, the greater the cost of benefits, which drives up liabilities (the cost of the plan).

Now, how about assets? Again, since the plan is obligated to a specific future payment, it is dependent on the assets and asset growth (investment returns) of the plan to meet those future obligations. So investment returns are the primary risk on the assets side.

Look at it this way: a plan's liabilities are not fixed but vary according to multiple factors, including those mentioned above.

And a plan's assets are dependent upon investment returns, which are also not fixed. What is fixed, however, is the amount promised to participants on a monthly basis. What, then, is the balancing item, but funding? If a plan has higher than expected liabilities, say through increased longevity of its retirees but lower than expected asset performance due to poor market performance and low interest rates, its funding requirement (how much the sponsor has to put into the plan) rises—perhaps significantly. A simple equation that represents the fundamental cost for all plans is: cost over a plan's lifetime = benefits paid + expenses associated with running the plan − investment income. While costs may vary year by year according to actuarial assumptions and methods, in the end, this equation holds true for all plans.

In the past 50 years, longevity has increased, on average, approximately 1.75 years per decade and we are all familiar with how investment returns have suffered recently. And to really put the scope of this issue into perspective, some DB plans have grown in size to as much as two and even three times the value of the companies that sponsored them. Managing the balance sheet volatility that results from sponsoring a DB plan has become a much larger dilemma. Again, to use our cross-town analogy, DB plans effectively hit a fire hydrant midtown, meaning most are underfunded. So much so that many companies have frozen or terminated their plans in favor of defined contribution plans, because with DC plans the funding requirements are more predictable and the investment risk is effectively shifted to the participant.

The Defined Benefit Myth

As we outlined in Chapter 2, DB plans began to mushroom in corporate America during the middle part of the twentieth century. According to the Employee Benefit Research Institute (EBRI), between 1940 and 1960 the number of people covered by private pensions increased from 3.7 million to 19 million, representing almost 30 percent of the labor force. By 1975, according to the Department of Labor, some 103,000 plans covered 33 million people in this country. Today, those figures look a little different. While the number of Americans covered has remained just north of 40 million, the number of DB plans stands at just over 47,000, and that number is steadily declining. But while the overall DB market is declining in numbers, one segment of DB plans is still growing. Small business owners, who realize they need to save more for retirement than the amount permitted in a DC plan, are turning to DB plans for their higher deferral limits.

It is important to note that being covered does not mean that a person has actually earned a benefit but only that they are covered in the event that they stay long enough at their company to be vested and be entitled to future benefits. As an employee of a company with a DB plan you are likely a covered participant on day one. However, DB plans are set up with a vesting schedule and usually take five years for a participant to become vested and to be entitled to their accrued benefit payments at retirement. Unfortunately, many employees don't stay long enough with a company for that to happen.

A common myth with respect to retirement plans is that in the good old days people worked for a company pretty much for their whole lives. The prevailing belief is that, in exchange for long-standing loyalty, paternalistic employers provided generous pension schemes so that when their employees retired they never had to worry about retirement income.

The heyday of the traditional, defined benefits era makes you long for those days to come back, doesn't it? Except that, on the whole, the image that everyone was covered by a DB plan turns out to be more of a myth than reality. As we pointed out in Chapter 2, even though the first corporate pension plan was created for employees of the American Express corporation in 1875, and the concept began to be more widely adopted, by 1932 only 15 percent of American workers had access to such plans, with only a small percentage of those actually receiving any payments.

Fast-forward to the latter half of the twentieth century and the experience of EBRI's Nevin Adams, as just one example. He worked for his first employer for nine years and was a participant in the company's DB plan. When he left that firm, his years of service resulted in no benefit at all, because the plan required employees to stay with the company for 10 years before they vested. That was a relatively short vesting schedule compared to earlier pension plans where longer vesting schedules of between 15 and 30 years of service were the norm.

Nevin continues, "I was with my second employer for 13 years and earned a benefit there, but didn't have the option of a lump-sum payout. So, when I'm 65, I think I'll be entitled to a pension of just over $200 a month."

That is not much to celebrate after a total of 22 years service with two employers, both of whom offered traditional pension plans, wouldn't you agree?

Ted Benna adds, "We tend to be very critical of our progress in getting people ready for retirement. There is this broadly held misconception that we used to have a lot better system than we do now. The reality is that this simply isn't true. I mean, going back to when I started in this business, the private retirement system was horrible. It was wretched. This was pre-ERISA and, to give you a specific example, I worked in the home office of an insurance company and they had a defined benefit pension plan. To become a participant in that plan, you had to be 30 if you were a male, 35 if you were a female, and you had to stay until you were age 60 before you had any vested benefit. That simply wouldn't work today."

Part of what makes this myth seem so realistic is that we are all convinced that back in the day most people worked their entire lives for just one or two companies. While it's predicted that the Millennials will have up to 10 careers in their lifetime, the cohort preceding the Baby Boomers (known as the Silent Generation, those born between 1925 and 1945) were thought to stay in one career, with one employer, pretty much the whole of their working lives. So, as the lore would have it, the average American worked at a job for 30-plus years then was compensated with a relaxed retirement, funded by an ironclad and generous monthly pension check.

But the job tenure myth also crumbles once you scratch the surface. According to EBRI's President and CEO, Dallas Salisbury, "Median job tenure has changed very little over the post-World War II era. It would likely surprise many to learn that the median job tenure of about five years has remained consistent, even when we reach all the way back to 1952—some 60 years." This directly refutes the conventional wisdom about lifetime employment.

As Nevin Adams explained, "When people think about defined benefit plans as a premise and a structure I think part of the problem is they look back to their childhood as being very *Leave It to Beaver* idyllic. But the truth is, everyone *didn't* have a pension. Most people never worked long enough, even if their company provided a pension plan, for them to accumulate any sort of significant benefit."

We make this point, not to undermine the perceived value of defined benefit plans, but rather to bring some balance to the discussion. Those of us who are lucky enough to have an accrued benefit in a traditional pension plan are very fortunate indeed, because this means we have the benefit of lifetime income at retirement, a benefit we will not outlive. The simple point we are making is that the problems of coverage and the accrued benefit are not new issues, but have been present since the inception of the pension plan.

For those who did stay with one company for the duration, there was much to commend DB plans. John Carl, president of Retirement Learning Center LLC told us how his father, after returning from fighting in World War II, maintained a long career at what was formerly Western Electric and later became Lucent Alcatel. "The only thing (my father) had to do to accrue his retirement benefit was show up to work. He didn't have to think about it. He didn't have to do anything else." But to get lulled into believing that Mr. Carl's experience was the norm would be to succumb to revisionist history.

The Rise of Defined Contribution Plans

What follows is not meant to be a comprehensive history of the rise of defined contribution (DC) plans. We acknowledge the contribution of landmark legislation—including the Economic Growth and Tax Relief Reconciliation Act (EGTRRA) of 2001 that introduced the Saver's Credit, among other initiatives, and the Pension Protection Act (PPA) of 2006 that contains safe harbors for auto-plan features—that are discussed later in this book. However, it is beyond our scope to give them more than a brief mention. For more in-depth coverage, the Investment Company Institute report entitled *401(k) Plans: A 25-Year Retrospective* is available online (see the Bibliography).

Suffice it to say that with respect to the earlier DB plans, the increasing demand of funding was largely responsible for their decline in popularity, with DC plans taking their place. What further fueled the migration from DB to DC plans was a section of the Revenue Act of 1978 stating that, "employees are not taxed on the portion of income they elect to receive as deferred compensation rather than as direct cash payments." Ted Benna, who later became known as the "father of the 401(k)," worked with Treasury regulators to pave the way for the advent of the 401(k) plan.

By 1981, the Internal Revenue Service (IRS) had proposed regulations on 401(k) plans that sanctioned the use of employee salary reductions as a source of contributions toward saving for retirement. Yet the 401(k) was never meant to become the primary means of saving for retirement.

Perhaps bolstered by the bull markets of the 1980s and 1990s, individuals welcomed the opportunity to reduce their tax liabilities and supplement their retirement savings. Indeed, the 401(k) opened up many new choices and freedoms to which the average American worker had not been exposed previously. They now had more control over the funds in their retirement plan, including the fact that, unlike defined benefit plans in which assets remain with the company, 401(k) plans were portable. Workers could take their own 401(k) assets plus any vested employer contributions with them as they moved from job to job, giving them greater flexibility to make changes in search of career advancement or higher salaries without the fear of losing their accumulated retirement benefits.

The creation of 401(k) plans was seen by both employers and employees as a win–win. The number of plans grew to the extent that EBRI's *History of 401(k) Plans* report from 2005 stated, "Within two years . . . nearly half of all large firms were either already offering a 401(k) plan or considering one." Some of that growth came from companies that froze their existing DB plans and began offering only 401(k) plans to their employees. The greatest impact, arguably, that this new approach made was to a broader coverage of retirement plans in the workplace.

As Brian Graff, CEO of the American Society of Pension Professionals and Actuaries (ASPPA) pointed out:

> At least now [the average American] has an opportunity to save that they never had before. The 401(k) has in some places been a replacement for the traditional defined benefit plan, but frankly it has opened up retirement savings to a huge section of the economy that didn't have that opportunity before, principally in small midsize companies. Those people never had a defined benefit plan. Now, at

least, they have a retirement plan that provides them with a meaningful opportunity to save.

That being said, it is important to note that the advent of the 401(k) plan did not actually reduce the risks outlined above in connection with DB plans. All of the challenges of reaching a funded DB plan continue to exist for DC plan participants in the defined contribution era, as we discuss next.

Changed Responsibilities

Despite the advantages of portability and control that 401(k) plans offered, can we really say with any certainty that all participants fully realized the responsibilities that came with them? After all, employees are now not only faced with shouldering the burden of deciding whether to participate in a plan and if so, at what level, they are also tasked with making wise investment choices.

The primary DB plan challenges of managing the assets and the liabilities of the plan in order to keep funding levels high enough to pay for future fixed benefits morphed when applied to DC plans. Remember, one of the most important distinctions between the DB plan and a DC plan is that while the DB plan defines the benefit (i.e., the amount paid to the retiree), the DC plan only defines the contribution (i.e., what the participant and employer pay into the plan). So, as a participant in a 401(k) plan, you decide how much you will put into the plan on a per paycheck basis—which is typically augmented by an employer match or profit sharing contribution—and then you have to determine how you will invest those assets, resulting in either good or poor asset performance. Based on those two decisions—how much you pay in and where you invest—you ideally end up with an account balance at retirement that outlives you. But that hinges on knowing how long that retirement period will last—something that none of us can say for certain.

Longevity

One of the primary differences between a DB and DC plan is that the risk of living too long is shifted from the employer to the employee.

While thinking about when you are likely to die is not a topic most of us like to address head-on, it's important when considering how much we need to accumulate in order to retire.

In the 1950s, when pension plans covered roughly a quarter of all employees working for big firms, the average 65-year-old retiree could expect to live another 13.9 years. Providing a lifetime retirement income for an employee back then was a realistic goal for most companies. However, today a 65-year-old man has a 40 percent chance of living to age 85 and a 20 percent chance of living to age 90. And a 65-year-old woman has a 53 percent chance of living to age 85 and a 31 percent chance of living to age 90. For a married couple, then, the chance of one of the spouses living longer than their life expectancy is significant.

Given the shift in responsibilities from employers to employees with respect to retirement readiness, we are now asking individuals—who have perhaps only started to fund their retirement in their late thirties or forties and have taken a hit on their savings because of the recent volatility of the stock market—to plan for the variability in the event they (or their spouse) live to be 90 or even older. And we are largely doing this without educating the average American on how to pool their longevity risk.

When you look at average life expectancy, that figure is basically useless for making any sort of informed decision about retirement, except at a very superficial level. As Jay Vivian pointed out, "We have everybody wishing that they could retire at 55 and live to 90. Wait, let me get this straight—you're going to start working at 20, and work for 35 years (until age 55) and then be retired for 35 years (age 90)? That model won't work unless you're going to save a huge part of your pay!"

Planning for an average life expectancy is fraught with problems, continues Jay Vivian: "Let's say somebody does look up the actuarial tables and realizes, oh, I'm supposed to live to be 86. So I'd better figure out my spending so that my money will last until I'm 86 because that's my life expectancy, right? Well, that's my *median* life expectancy. So, if I plan my spending so my money runs out when I turn 86, that means that for every 100 people who do what I'm doing, half of us are going to have to eat cat food. And the other half are going to die with too much money."

One answer, at least for some, might be to pool that longevity risk with a product such as an annuity where the risk doesn't go away but gets redistributed among everyone in the plan. The benefit of an annuity is that if you are planning for a lifetime of, say, 86 years and you actually live to be 100, you get 14 additional years—none of them involving making the choice between health care and dinner! Like life insurance, the additional benefits drawn by those who live longer than the average are covered by those who do not.

The irony is, most 401(k)s had annuity options. When you came to retire you were typically offered a lump sum to invest as you saw fit, or an annuity that meant you would get a set amount every month for the rest of your life. Unfortunately, given that annuities are conservative, low-yielding investments, few people wanted anything to do with them during the bull market years. That, coupled with requirements for additional paperwork and signatures, caused many companies to simply stop offering the annuity option.

Yet annuities are by no means the only solution to the risk of outliving one's income. The fact is, the evolution of the 401(k) has been largely driven by demand and, until recently, there has been little demand for anything other than a lump-sum payout from these plans. But as life expectancies have extended and 401(k)s have taken on a more significant role in the retirement readiness of Americans, the demand for a solution to the longevity risk quandary has increased and new solutions are being put forward.

As Brian Graff pointed out: "I think annuities definitely have their place, but I'm not necessarily saying it has to be an annuity. There are lots of creative things that we can do, but we don't. That's because DC plans have really been designed to accumulate assets, not to give them away."

So, if we now live in a time when voluntary savings coupled with mandatory Social Security are meant to prepare us for retirement, and participants, not employers, need to make important decisions regarding funding, investments, and protecting against longevity, how have voluntary workplace retirement plans evolved to better serve us?

The Evolution of 401(k)

The early 401(k) plan market was a far cry from what it is today. Most plans offered few investment choices and limited ability to move between them. For example, Section 404(c), which was added to ERISA on October 13, 1992, offered employers relief from the liability that resulted from their employees' investment selections if they followed set guidelines. These guidelines included offering employees a minimum of three investments with varying risk/reward characteristics and the ability to shift between them on a quarterly basis.

Today, when accounts are web-based and traded daily, and investment choices can be virtually unlimited, a plan with only three investment choices and the ability to trade on a quarterly basis would be a real dinosaur. Plan sponsors now have investment policy statements, investment due diligence processes, and committees that make decisions about which investments to include in their investment menus. And today, participants enjoy flexibility and control over their investments like never before, but all of this is weighed against the average American having insufficient financial knowledge with which to make informed investment decisions.

Adding to that challenge, let's factor in the question of whether having more choices is actually better for the average participant. Research indicates that if the average worker is given too much choice they simply freeze or are likely to make poor decisions. It's a documented phenomenon that as investment menus extend beyond a manageable number of choices, the quality of decision-making is negatively impacted. Increasingly, recently hired participants are gravitating toward one-stop target date investments, indicating their preference for simplicity. This phenomenon is discussed further in Chapter 7. As Shlomo Benartzi points out in his book *Save More Tomorrow,* most people don't want the responsibility of making the sort of complex financial decisions that they have difficulty understanding, let alone making with any degree of confidence.

According to John Mott of Morgan Stanley Smith Barney:

For so long, there has been a certain portion of the older generation that has been used to companies doing things for them, and I think it's taking a long time for them to get to the point where they know they need to take care of themselves. What's interesting to me is that we had this 1960s generation that started the revolution, who wanted to do everything on their own and be in control, but when it came to their finances—which is one of the most important parts of maintaining your lifestyle—most refused to want to deal with that for such a long time.

Yet, in their defense, we have to say that it is hardly surprising that most people are not engaged with the topic of retirement readiness and find the act of investing (which retirement planning has evolved into, rather than simply saving) to be intimidating. Thankfully we are now seeing an increasing call for automatic plan features and for the pendulum to swing back from complexity to simplicity.

Rather than asking people to choose whether or not to join a plan and where to invest their accounts, there is a growing belief within the retirement plan industry that changing to auto-enrollment and defaulting assets into an age/risk appropriate investment is the way to go—two of the topics we cover in more detail in Chapter 7. This means that employees are defaulted into behaviors that have a higher probability of retirement readiness. Consistent with maintaining flexibility and personal choice, those who wish to take on more responsibility and venture outside of the defaults are still free to do so and have ample information and guidance to help them make informed decisions.

Just let's not blame the 401(k) system or claim—as some do—that 401(k)s have failed. According to Mike DiCenso, the overall structure, administration, and recordkeeping, even the investment side of 401(k)s are not what has failed: "The individual participant's education, knowledge, and their proactive utilization of the plan—that's what's failed."

What if we took financial literacy more seriously in order to help the average American better understand how much they need to save and what it means for them when they do retire? Might we then solve the retirement readiness issue? These are the questions we explore next.

Chapter 5

Financial Literacy

The number one problem in today's generation and economy is the lack of financial literacy.

—Alan Greenspan

Santiago Martinez (not his real name) and his spouse have two children, aged 3 and 15. Their combined annual income is $25,000, an average figure for the area of Texas in which they live. Each month they must cover their apartment rent, insurance, car payment, plus things like cell phone, food, and cable. When their teenage son decides to sneak out with the family car to go to a party and crashes it into a tree, they need to find $150 to pay the local hospital for his stitches. After some discussion, Santiago realized it wasn't worth claiming this relatively small amount on the family's insurance since it would only raise their rates. By picking up a few extra shifts at work he was able to make enough to cover that unexpected cost and add an extra $50 to the money the family tries to save every month.

Santiago is really only 18 years old and this isn't real life for him, but it soon could be. He is a student participant in a personal finance game developed by Mathew Frost, who teaches American history and economics to eleventh and twelfth graders at Sunset High School in Dallas, where the 2200 students are largely Hispanic. In college, Mathew had been exposed to a similar game devised by one of his sociology professors. So when the state legislature in Texas determined that personal finance was to be incorporated into the high school curriculum, Mathew took the basics of his former professor's idea and turned it into a highly interactive classroom experience.

The game works like this. Each student is hypothetically paired up as a married couple on an annual income that matches to some degree the community in which they currently live. They start out with two children but could end up facing another pregnancy before the game is over. Similar to the way that the board game *Monopoly* incorporates Chance and Community Chest cards, the student teams pull cards representing random life events—good and bad. One month they might face a rent increase, on another they might get a bonus at work. A relative might die and leave them a small inheritance, or one of their children has a birthday and asks for a Nintendo Wii. There is also a won-the-lottery card that only one lucky participant has pulled in the four years that Mathew has been offering this course as part of the economics curriculum.

The winning group is the one with the most money saved at the end of the 12 cycles (one cycle representing each month of a year, although the exercise extends over just 6 weeks of the 18-week semester); winners are certainly never in debt.

On one occasion, a team whose annual income had been set at $22,000 managed to at least save something because they had researched a federal program—Temporary Assistance for Needy Families—and found that they were eligible for $1,500 worth of monthly benefits. It is this kind of personal initiative that Mathew Frost looks to develop in his students, in addition to persuading them to save some of the money they otherwise would have had to find for food, health care, and other family costs.

Stressing a point that was made to us many times by various retirement industry experts we interviewed, Mathew adds that, "Some families in the game—like Santiago's—that make less money generally do better at saving than those with middle-class incomes who will spend what they have and then find when they pull a card for an event that they were not expecting have nothing set aside to cover that."

Is Mathew Frost moving the needle with respect to preparing his students for the financial challenges they will soon face in the real world? Absolutely. He knows that standing in front of his students talking about opportunity costs and other terms favored by economists is just going to turn off these young people. So he engages them emotionally with a true-to-life game that helps to capture their imaginations and provokes initiative. At its core, his approach isn't about filling their heads with context-independent information that they'll forget in a heartbeat, it's about developing critical thinking skills that will help them make good decisions over time.

Mathew's game also instills in students the confidence to see that financial acumen is something they can easily acquire and further develop. In short, he helps to change their *beliefs*. What he faces, however, is often an uphill battle—not least from a lack of parental guidance around saving.

On the home front, for example, one of his female students was being given $100 a week allowance from her father. Since she was planning to go to college, Mathew asked her if she was saving any of that money (a not insubstantial $5,200 a year). She began to do exactly that, until her mother found out that she was saving the money instead of spending it and that allowance was suddenly cut back. What message does that send?

Time is also an issue for teachers like Mathew, who are caught between teaching a course that will impact the financial decisions these students may be making in just a few months' time and other required coursework. But, then again, is there ever enough time in the school year to accomplish all that we would ideally want? With respect to Mathew Frost's other teaching subject, for example, he's given 36 weeks to cover 280 years of American history.

During the first year that personal finance was introduced into the economics curriculum in Mathew's school, the course lasted just two weeks. Nevertheless, that's an improvement on the one-hour workplace enrollment meetings that are often the first opportunity most American adults have to think about budgeting and saving for retirement. But, as Joe Mrozek shared with us, "It is beyond comprehension that today, in America, we don't do a better job of prioritizing financial literacy in our schools. Neither my 17-year-old nor my 12-year-old twins have been exposed to this critical topic in school in any meaningful way. How is that possible in this day and age?" Joe is absolutely right; we have to do better.

Defining Financial Literacy

Let's start by addressing what we mean by financial literacy.

To our interviewees in the retirement industry, the definition of financial literacy as it relates to retirement readiness means going beyond simple budgeting but not as far as having to know the intricacies of stocks and bonds. What it definitely involves, in their minds, is the need for people to know enough about their retirement savings and other financial matters in order to make good decisions over time.

As Nevin Adams pointed out—and the reason why he feels that the auto-enrollment approach *by itself* is not the answer—retirement decisions are not single events, like buying a house.

When you are making a house purchase:

> . . . *hopefully you're bringing on people and hiring at a certain level of expertise and they're helping you get through the morass so you make the right decisions. Then you're done with it. You've got your house, you're paying your mortgage, and that's it for the time being.*

> *The problem with retirement decisions is that you don't just do it once. I think we could absolutely teach everybody in America to make that first good investment savings decision. The challenge is, how do we get them to revisit that first good decision and do it on a regular basis?*

There is no doubt that financial literacy and retirement readiness are strongly correlated, as identified in studies conducted globally by Annamaria Lusardi, Director of the Global Center for Financial Literacy at the George Washington School of Business. Echoing the quote by Alan Greenspan that opened this chapter, Lusardi points out: "Just as it was not possible to live in an industrialized society without print literacy—the ability to read and write—so it is not possible to live in today's world without being financially literate. To fully participate in society today financial literacy is critical."

But achieving financial literacy is not just about access to more information. It is about knowing what to do with the information you are presented with.

Which brings us back to the concept of critical thinking, defined by the National Council for Excellence in Critical Thinking as: ". . . the

intellectually disciplined process of actively and skillfully concep-
tualizing, applying, analyzing, synthesizing, and/or evaluating
information gathered from, or generated by, observation, experience,
reflection, reasoning, or communication, as a guide to belief
and action."

Anyone familiar with the classification of educational learning
goals and objectives known as Bloom's Taxonomy will recognize
that critical thinking involves higher levels of cognition than simply
being able to remember or summarize facts and figures. At its
culmination, critical thinking is the ability to judge information,
determine your options, and give weight to one choice over another.
It is one thing to remember and understand the information you may
have come across about savings in general or retirement readiness
in particular—through initiatives ranging from *Feed the Pig* to the
National Retirement Planning Coalition's *Retire on Your Terms*. It's
quite another thing to evaluate that information in order to create a
personalized savings and retirement plan that works for your life and
unique needs.

We don't need to be trying to educate people to the elevated level
that Paul D'Auitolo describes as beyond the capabilities even of those
who work generally in the retirement services industry:

> *If you look at institutional consulting at its core, all those pools of*
> *money are historically run by very sophisticated investment*
> *committees that have to make choices on asset allocation, have to*
> *make choices on managers, have to make choices on a lot of*
> *different things. What we've done in asking the average participant*
> *to fund their own pension plan is to expect them to have skills that*
> *are the equivalent of an institutional consultant paired with a*
> *sophisticated investment committee in order to make the right*
> *choices. It's asinine to think that any participant can do that.*

In a sense, the issue of retirement readiness is no different to any of
the ongoing challenges we have in a world in which it makes less
sense to focus our educational efforts on *what* (as in cramming heads
full of information that may be irrelevant or inaccurate very quickly),
and requires a greater focus on helping people find their own answers
to *why* and *how*.

Kent Callahan, CEO of Transamerica Employer Solutions and Pensions, adds:

> *People focus on things that are important to them when they're important to them and not before. A 21-year-old is not going to spend a lot of time thinking about retirement readiness. But a 35-year-old with $41,000 in his account is now going to engage and spend more time. As his savings grow, it becomes more and more important and that's when he will begin to pull information from the system. So we need to prepare people for that time, by getting their savings habit started, by teaching them the basics of saving and investing, and by teaching them to think. At least then, when they're ready to pull what they need, they will actually understand it.*

Unfortunately, the first exposure that most people have to any kind of practical planning for retirement is during the workplace one-hour enrollment meeting which, for many of us, is too little too late.

Which brings us back to needing to do more in the home and in our schools.

In January 2008, President George W. Bush established the President's Advisory Council on Financial Literacy with the mission "to promote and enhance financial literacy" with a view to "help keep America competitive and assist the American people in understanding and addressing financial matters."

President Obama then signed an executive order creating the President's Advisory Council on Financial Capability in January 2010, again with the aim of helping Americans make "informed financial decisions and thereby contribute to financial stability." Part of what this Council addresses are "new approaches to increase financial capability through financial education. . . ."

Were you aware of either of these initiatives before now? Have any young people you know been exposed to a booklet entitled *Money As You Grow: 20 Things Kids Need to Know to Live Financially Smart Lives*, containing suggestions for activities that parents can engage in with their children at age-appropriate milestones, for example?

Was anyone you know one of the 84,372 students from 1,692 public schools who participated in the 2011 National Financial Capability Challenge?

Shouldn't it alarm us that according to the Council for Economic Education's *Survey of the States: Economic and Personal Finance Education in Our Nation's Schools 2011* report, the trend toward teaching these critical life skills "is slowing and in some cases moving backwards."

Consider that in 2012, less than half of America (22 states—up from 21 in 2009) requires high school students to take courses in economics, and fewer still require those students to be tested in that subject. Even fewer states (14—one less than in 2009) require schools to offer a course in personal finance.

The majority of today's college seniors are graduating with an average of $25,250 in school loan debt, yet many of them will never have been exposed to the commonsense advice outlined in the booklet *Money as You Grow*. The concept of waiting before you buy something you *want* in order to first cover the things that you *need* is also a key issue that Mathew Frost inculcates in his students.

But there is another issue we should not overlook, and it's one that we raised with our interviewees: Who is qualified to teach personal finance in schools? Less than 20 percent of teachers report that they feel competent to teach this topic to their students, which may reflect the fact that the average American is so poorly prepared in this regard that fewer than half of us (49.7 percent) know what is meant by the term *budget deficit*.

Luckily that is not a problem for the students accessing the personal finance course at Sunset High School in Dallas, Texas where Mathew Frost teaches. Frost has a strong sense of personal responsibility when it comes to finance and can articulate this to his students. After graduating from college in 2007, he started work as a data processor for a mutual fund company, before giving way to his passion and entering the teaching profession. Not only that, but he has clearly managed his own money well—from the time when his parents required him to earn his own money from cutting grass in order to buy his first television set, to saving a set amount from his teacher's salary every month in a retirement plan.

So here is another question: What opportunities might there be for the 401(k) Whisperers in the retirement and finance industries to teach the topic of personal finance and retirement readiness? In which case, public and private school teachers don't necessarily have to try to learn and understand all that these industry experts already know from years of first-hand experience.

At its core, this issue pivots around something Chad Larsen pointed out—which is contrary to how most curricula is developed:

> *I know what they don't need to know. To be financially literate and retirement ready you don't need to know the difference between large-cap and mid-cap stocks. I don't think anyone needs to know the difference between Treasury Inflation-Protected Securities (TIPS) and intermediate-term bonds. What the average American does need to know about and focus on is the amount of their contribution to a retirement fund. That's what's going to have the greatest impact on their ability to retire, not whether they picked the right fund or the wrong fund or all those things that we spend the vast majority of our time on.*

Of course, as Ted Benna commented to us, even if we were able to get agreement on this, we would need to address the issue of "What kind of consistency might you have?" But that is focusing on the tactical stuff of curriculum development and needs to play a secondary role to the strategically focused outcome we are all looking to achieve: a nation of financially literate individuals who not only secure their own futures but contribute to the overall economic security and functioning of American society over time.

Making Saving Stick

So, given that this book is more about asking the right questions than providing any pat answers, let us ask you this. As an educator, industry specialist—or as a parent—what perspective do you have about how to improve the reach, standards, and life-long impact of financial literacy through the teaching of personal finance courses in our schools (and for more on this issue, see the Letters to Stakeholders in Chapter 11)?

In a fast-paced, ever-changing world, the average American needs to know enough to make the right financial decisions at the right time, according to their individual aspirations and needs. And we need to make that learning palatable . . . in the same way that Mathew Frost is doing for his students. He describes what they take away from his course:

> We talk about making a budget and then we go to the game and they have to make a budget. And they have to do this for every month of the year so it's repeating the lesson over and over again. And then we talk about investing, when they get the option of whether or not to save their money in a savings account or put it somewhere they can't touch it. From that they learn how much they need to keep on hand for everyday needs and emergencies. I tell them they're not going to get interest on their savings until the end of the game and that introduces them to the notion of compound interest. And I've actually given them negative interest on investments in order to reflect what we've seen recently in the markets. I find a lot of students will put 10 or 15 percent of their savings every month into an investment account and keep the rest in their savings accounts just in case something happens. So in the game my students learn to save for that just-in-case moment.

And does that learning on budgeting stick?

A year after she attended his personal finance course, a young single mother who worked two jobs in addition to going to school emailed her former teacher to say that she was still working on her budget, tracking everything she spends within a spreadsheet the way that Mathew taught them to do. When students like her discover that they're spending thousands of dollars a year on a hobby when it could be put to better use elsewhere, they come around to changing their habits over time. And one of those habits needs to be that the more they earn the more they should save, rather than spending it on experiences or items that don't enhance their lives in the long term.

Which wasn't the case for one of Mathew's adult friends who is "really into firearms" and, having recently stepped into a higher paying job, planned to spend $1,000 on a rifle with his first paycheck—despite still being in the job's probationary period. As Mathew pointed out, "Heaven forbid he loses his job; then he has a $1,000 paperweight that nobody's going to give him that money for."

But how many of us know someone who makes frivolous purchases—or have even done things like that ourselves? Maybe if we'd had the chance to learn about personal finance in school, would we still engage in these kinds of spur-of-the-moment behaviors?

In 2007, poet Jonathan Reed entered a two-minute video in AARP's U@50 contest, for which he won second place. Participants had to describe what they expected their life to be like when they turned 50. Inspired by the Argentinean political campaign advertisement, "The Truth," Reed wrote and recorded "Lost Generation" which, on the face of it, reads like an indictment of today's quick-fix society, with the voiceover speaking of a younger generation that is "apathetic and lethargic" and for whom "it is foolish to presume that there is hope."

Except, that's not the message you get when you read each of the sentences in reverse order. Reading the poem backwards, it actually *celebrates* belief in a new era, one in which family trumps work and true happiness isn't about money but what lies within. Take a look:

Read Forward:

I am part of a lost generation and
I refuse to believe that I can change the world.
I realize this may be a shock but
"Happiness comes from within"
is a lie, and
"Money will make me happy"
So in 30 years I will tell my children
they are not the most important thing in my life
My employer will know that
I have my priorities straight because
work
is more important than
family.
I tell you this
once upon a time
families stayed together
but this will not be true in my era
This is a quick fix society.
experts tell me
30 years from now I will be celebrating the 10th anniversary of my divorce
I do not concede that
I will live in a country of my own making
In the future

Environmental destruction will be the norm
No longer can it be said that
My peers and I care about this earth
It will be evident that
My generation is apathetic and lethargic
It is foolish to presume that
There is hope.

And all of this will come true unless we choose to reverse it.

Read Backward:
There is hope.
It is foolish to presume that
My generation is apathetic and lethargic
It will be evident that
My peers and I care about this earth
No longer can it be said that
Environmental destruction will be the norm
In the future
I will live in a country of my own making
I do not concede that
30 years from now I will be celebrating the 10th anniversary
of my divorce
Experts tell me
this is a quick fix society
but this will not be true in my era
Families stayed together
Once upon a time
I tell you this
family
is more important than
work
I have my priorities straight because
My employer will know that
they are not the most important thing in my life
So in 30 years I will tell my children
"Money will make me happy"
is a lie and
"Happiness comes from within"
I realize this may be a shock but I can change the world and
I refuse to believe that I am part of a lost generation.

This is analogous to where we stand today with respect to financial literacy. As we have stated repeatedly (and will continue to do so throughout the rest of this book), we have done a decent job in this country of getting the 401(k) to be taken seriously and we are starting to see the benefits from the many contextual factors that have been put in place to remind people of the value of saving for their retirement.

But in order to reverse the current trend and experience a happier state of affairs—if not for the current generation of retirees, then for future ones—we must also address the issue of beliefs.

Remarkable, passionate, and appropriately experienced teachers like Mathew Frost are doing just that—reinforcing the beliefs of their students so they can prepare themselves and financially plan for the real-life situations that currently surprise far too many of us and detrimentally impact the little financial security we might have. But are there enough of these exceptional teachers in today's schools, and are we helping or hindering their efforts?

At the end of Mathew's personal finance class, the students are asked to write a two-page paper covering just three things:

1. Tell a story about what happened during this experience.
2. What did you learn?
3. How would you change the game to make it better?

As another of his students, Bonita Garcia (not her real name), wrote in part:

> *I know that the decisions we made in the game weren't that bad, but they weren't as thought through as they should have been. We should have saved more and part of that was not coming up with a better budget. I recommend this game to all high school students, not just ones studying economics. It helped me organize my future financial planning and better understand what it means to spend less and save more. I learned that needs must always come before wants no matter what. I would like to take part in this project again next year if possible. I appreciate all that this project has taught me and I will never forget what I learned about budgeting.*

In terms of our focus on the relationship between context and beliefs, it is clear that it is not enough simply to draw attention to the issue of financial literacy by introducing the topic into our schools. Such efforts, like Mathew Frost's, need to be motivational and structured in such a way that they help to change individual beliefs.

Tackling beliefs at this personal level is still not sufficient. What we need to do, if any retirement readiness initiative is truly going to move the needle, is to effect change at the wider, societal level.

How might we do that? To answer that question we looked for inspiration at some of the most effective advertising campaigns in U.S. history to discover how they not only changed behavior but in some cases completely reshaped our cultural norms.

Chapter 6

Lessons Learned, Changing Outcomes

The underlying theme was that the social change required to bring women into the workforce was a patriotic responsibility for women and employers.

—Rosie the Riveter campaign, Ad Council website

Let us imagine for the moment that we already have a long-running, highly popular retirement readiness campaign that has significantly boosted the number of Americans who are saving more for the time when they are no longer able or willing to work. Thanks to the success of this campaign we have largely circumnavigated the problem where millions of Americans are living longer without the means to support themselves. In short, we have successfully accomplished what we set out to do: to change behavior so the average person's money outlives them, not the other way around.

Why isn't there a campaign like that?

Certainly there is plenty of information already out there acting as both carrot (here's what you need to do) and stick (here's where we're headed if things don't change soon). The Information Age offers both good and bad news on another score: it could be that the overwhelming amount of information across multiple, often contradictory, channels is stifling action. We don't need *more* information. What we need is a way to articulate a clear message that tells people only what is really necessary, showing them how to use that information, and weaving it in such a way that they are strongly motivated to do so.

What we need is a national campaign that's sticky enough to change beliefs and actions. How do we do that?

Disrupting Thinking

Communication experts know that people don't adopt new behaviors simply from having easier access to more information. Much more than that is needed.

All successful advertising campaigns need to be persuasive and are designed with these elements: here's what I have for you, here's what it will do for you, here's who we are (so you can trust us), and here's what you need to do next (the call to action).

For such a campaign to reach the widest number of people, it would benefit from being backed by a wide range of key constituencies. It is not enough for this to be a retirement services industry-only effort, for several reasons.

Perhaps most importantly, we need to involve everyone, not only to reinforce that this is a social not an industry-specific issue, but also because—as Albert Einstein once famously said, "We can't solve problems with the same thinking we used when we created them." Yet we know how hard it is for people, especially experts who have been close to a specific topic for a very long time, to change the way they think. We spend a great deal of time (10,000 hours, according to Malcolm Gladwell in *Outliers: The Story of Success*) developing and embedding our expertise or value proposition. Being willing to change the perspective on which that expertise was built is something many people are resistant to do.

As Fielding Miller, CEO of CAPTRUST Financial Advisors, points out:

> *Being actively involved in providing participant education and advice affords a healthy reminder of what the world looks like for most employees. Building a sufficient retirement savings is an elusive goal for most American workers, especially those on the lower end of the income scale. Over the past several years we have seen many failed attempts aimed at improving outcomes—whether increasing savings, better investing, or basic retirement planning. I believe these failures are mostly due to the myopic orientation of the*

financial service industry, which has been disconnected from the real customer, the participant. Improving outcomes starts with our willingness to get out there and go eye to eye with the single mom working the third shift at the textile plant. There is no substitute for this type of connection—it keeps us grounded and focused on the main event: creating solutions that improve outcomes for everyone.

As the founder of the World Innovation Institute, entrepreneur, and philanthropist Naveen Jain articulated in *Forbes* when writing online about disruptive innovation:

I believe that people who will come up with creative solutions to solve the world's biggest problem —ecological devastation, global warming, the global debt crisis and distribution of dwindling natural resources, to name a few—will NOT be experts in their fields. The real disruptors will be those individuals who are not steeped in one industry of choice, with those coveted 10,000 hours of experience, but instead, individuals who approach challenges with a clean lens, bringing together diverse experiences, knowledge, and opportunities.

Another reason why we need to open up the retirement readiness debate is because of the skepticism with which many people view any solely industry- or business-led initiatives. Take the Keep America Beautiful (KAB) campaign that spawned the Crying Indian PSA, for example. Look online and you can read the considerable criticism that ensued because of who funded it: bottlers, fast food companies, and other packaging manufacturers. It seems that regardless of the success Keep America Beautiful had in helping to bring attention to the problem of littering and pollution, some commentators never saw beyond the controversial aspects of the campaign. These included the belief (at least in the mind of detractors) that the KAB campaign diverted attention away from the responsibilities of the packaging manufacturers who had been facing legislation to create more expensive, reusable containers, rather than disposable ones. Their argument was that the Keep America Beautiful campaign shifted the onus onto consumers by telling them it was *their* responsibility to clear up their litter, rather than requiring different standards from the manufacturers in terms of the excessive packaging they produced.

Similarly, if we were to tackle retirement readiness from only a financial services industry perspective it is highly likely that we would face the same kind of skepticism that was leveled at the KAB campaign, with critics assuming that we were doing this just to try and sell products and services, and line their own pockets.

That is why the campaign we are proposing needs to be broader than any single company or even the industry as a whole. It needs the support of government and employers, as well as community groups and other organizational stakeholders.

Campaign Role Models

Before we even get into the issue of support, though, the question remains: what would such a campaign, offering a compelling message around retirement readiness, look like?

In order to answer that question, we looked to various public service announcements for inspiration. We wanted to go beyond a single campaign—such as Keep America Beautiful—in order to explore more deeply how these approaches have fundamentally changed American behaviors and social norms. The additional campaigns we investigated were: Rosie the Riveter, Smokey Bear, Click It Or Ticket, and Smoking Is Ugly.

The choice of which of the many anti-smoking campaigns to investigate highlights subtlety around public communication campaigns that is useful for us to address at the outset.

As Julia Coffman points out in her 2002 Harvard Family Research Project paper entitled *Public Communication Campaign Evaluation: An Environmental Scan of Challenges, Criticisms, Practice, and Opportunities,* there are two types of public-will campaigns: those that mobilize action in order to influence and change policy, and those that are designed either to eliminate antisocial or problematic behaviors in individuals, or shape desired behaviors that not only benefit the person but also help to change social norms. Such campaigns are designed not just to influence a person's resolve to act, but need to identify very specifically what the new behavior should look like.

For example, in the case of two very different anti-smoking campaigns, an organization like The Truth (www.thetruth.com) is focused on influencing policy, with the target being the tobacco industry. As they state on their website: "Our philosophy isn't anti-smoker or pro-smoker. It's not even about smoking. It's about the tobacco industry manipulating their products, research, and advertising to secure 'replacements' for the 1200 customers they 'lose' everyday in America. You know, because they die."

Contrast that message with model Christy Turlington's Smoking Is Ugly campaign that is focused on showing teenagers the undesirable consequences (bad breath, smelly clothing, stained teeth) of smoking cigarettes. Both are focused on the issue of smoking, but from different perspectives, and as such provoke different kinds of action. The Truth is lobbying against the tobacco industry, presumably to stop the manufacture of cigarettes, while Turlington wants to persuade the appearance-conscious teenager not to smoke.

The perspective that we are focusing on regarding the retirement readiness issue is that of individual behavior change, not policy, which is how we selected the following five classic campaigns listed in chronological order below. You are probably familiar with most, if not all, of them—but here's a quick refresher, including the Keep America Beautiful campaign that we introduced at the beginning of the book.

ROSIE THE RIVETER (1942–1945)

Before Rosie was launched on the national stage, the social norm in America was for married women to work in the home. Regardless of what career they may have had before marriage, afterwards their primary responsibility was to keep house and bring up children. World War II changed all that. With so many men fighting overseas, there was a shortage of workers who could "man" the factories and assembly lines. These jobs were vital to the war effort, principally the munitions and aircraft industries. Those available to fill vacant positions were mainly women.

The motivational message of "We Can Do It!" illustrated by an attractive woman in overalls flexing her muscles, was clearly aimed at female patriotism. Specific messages included: "The more women at work, the sooner we win," with women being reminded that by supporting the war effort in this way they were more likely to get their men home quicker.

Aside from the colorful Rosie posters, magazines that were enjoying increased circulations played a big part in spreading this message.

Norman Rockwell even drew the cover for the *Saturday Evening Post's* Memorial Day 1943 issue that featured the Rosie image.

There was no avoiding the message. And millions of women answered the call, swelling the number of American workers focused on the war effort by 2 million, according to the Ad Council that was responsible for designing the campaign and had been sponsored by the Office of War Information and War Manpower Commission.

The question of whether women had the strength and other capacities to take on these jobs was addressed by government advertisements that pointed out that if a woman could use an electric mixer, then she could operate a drill! Pictures and newsreels of women operating lathes, welding parts at steel plants, and handling jackhammers went hand in hand with the arguably less onerous task of fastening rivets on aircraft. If anyone had been in any doubt as to what the "little woman at home" was capable of doing on the factory floor, the millions of real-life Rosie the Riveters put an end to all that. Unfortunately, it took a war to spur that social change.

This campaign did not just galvanize the war effort at home by recruiting vital workers; it completely changed the social climate. Women now knew what they were capable of and the war effort undoubtedly influenced the second wave of the feminist movement that began in the early 1960s. The daughters of wartime women had very compelling role models who could show them how women could take their place in a wide range of workplaces—not just the factory floor.

Smokey Bear (1944–Present)

Wildfires had always been a problem for the U.S. Forest Service but, as with Rosie, World War II provoked a new urgency to curb their effects. The Japanese military had attempted to ignite many West Coast forests with a weapon known as the *Fu-Go*—balloon bombs that could be released from ships and aircraft. The idea behind these activities was to create panic and show Americans that attacks weren't restricted to Pearl Harbor—we could be attacked at home too. It has been estimated that something like 1,000 of these fire balloons actually reached the U.S. coast. Although the threat of these Fu-Go bombs was kept fairly low-key by the authorities—they worried about widespread panic—news channels reported that five children and their teacher had been killed as they approached one of these fire bombs that had landed, without previously exploding, in a forest in Oregon.

Prior to Smokey, the Disney organization had allowed characters including Bambi to be used in forest fire prevention campaigns. When that agreement expired, another cute animal messenger needed to be found; thus, Smokey Bear was born.

As with Rosie, the behavior required of Americans in relation to this campaign was very simple and specific. Instead of "go to work" it was to prevent wildfires by avoiding the human thoughtlessness that is responsible for so much of this destruction. "Remember—only YOU can prevent forest fires," was one of the earlier slogans; messages have been modified over the years.

Given that Smokey is the longest running campaign in Ad Council history, it is almost certain that most of you have been exposed to these messages in some shape or form. In addition to posters, there have been cartoons, comic strips, dolls, books, and other paraphernalia all dedicated to promoting the message of Smokey: be careful not to inadvertently start a fire when you are anywhere near dry vegetation.

As a result of this mass-media focus, the Smokey Bear campaign is credited with having reduced the number of acres lost annually from 22 million acres—an area equivalent to the size of Maine—to 8.4 million acres, according to the most recent (2000) figures given by the Ad Council.

KEEP AMERICA BEAUTIFUL (1961–1983)

Right up to the end of World War II in the United States, buying a soda pop typically meant purchasing a glass bottle from a store to which you could return the empty container for a refill or receive a small deposit back. In 1947, according to the Institute for Local Self-Reliance's website, the market share for carbonated soft drinks in refillable glass bottles was 100 percent; by 2000 this had dropped to less than 1 percent.

In the intervening period, the benefits of one-way containers—not just for soda but a wide range of products—were being promoted: consumers were now freed up from having to store and return empty bottles; retailers no longer had to manage the return of deposits; and bottle manufacturers did not have to maintain wash and inspection sites to deal with all the bottles that came back to them.

Very soon, however, the question became: what do we do about the increase in littering as a result of the trend for selling beverages (among other things) in aluminum cans and nonreturnable plastic or glass bottles?

In 1953, Vermont offered its response by enacting a ban on the sale of beer in nonrefillable bottles. That was the year in which, according to the Keep America Beautiful website: "(A) group of corporate and civic leaders met in New York City to discuss a revolutionary idea—bringing the public and private sectors together to develop and promote a national cleanliness ethic."

The KAB's first Public Service Announcement (PSA) appeared shortly after, in 1956. But it wasn't until the coalition—which included business interests like Coca-Cola, PepsiCo, Philip Morris, and Anheuser-Busch as well as then First Lady, Lady Bird Johnson—began their collaboration with the Ad Council that their advertising messages began to pack a more powerful punch.

As Heather Rogers points out in her book *Gone Tomorrow: The Hidden Life of Garbage*, "the United States is the planet's number-one producer of trash," and packaging represents one third of that (see Plumer, *The Origins of Anti-Litter Campaigns*), so there has never been a lack of littering opportunities in this country. Enter The Crying Indian, the wake-up call to Americans that we described at length earlier in this book and which provoked more of us to pay attention to the harm we were doing to the environment.

This award-winning PSA, alongside the community-led, statewide, and federal initiatives that occurred in its wake, helped to make a dent in the littering statistics. According to one study funded by the KAB: "The actual count of overall litter is down by 61 percent since 1969," with a reduction in littering of beverage containers of almost 75 percent.

CLICK IT OR TICKET (1993–PRESENT)

Since the crash test dummies Vince and Larry were introduced to the American public in 1985 to advocate the use of safety belts in cars (they were finally retired in 1999), "usage has increased from 14 percent to 79 percent, saving an estimated 85,000 lives, and $3.2 billion in costs to society," according to the Ad Council.

In 1993 the baton was picked up by various states, starting with North Carolina, with the Click It Or Ticket campaign that is now mobilized countrywide by the National Highway Traffic Safety Administration (NHTSA).

Seat belt usage is an issue where the laws differ from state to state. Thirty-two states, plus DC and various U.S. territories, uphold what are known as primary seat belt laws, meaning that law enforcement officers can stop non-compliant drivers and issue tickets without any other traffic offense taking place. In the 17 states with secondary seat belt laws, there has to be another citable traffic infraction before law enforcement officers can issue a ticket for not wearing a seat belt.

The change in behavior required was so simple that, today, wearing seat belts is an accepted social norm across America, although campaigns like these continue to be funded because of the ease with which we can fall back into bad habits if we are not constantly reminded of how important it is to buckle up.

SMOKING IS UGLY (2010–PRESENT)

If there is any issue that lends itself to some of the most graphic and frightening visuals being seen in advertising today, it is smoking. The Smoking Is Ugly campaign, spearheaded by the World Health Organization and Centers for Disease Control and Prevention, and launched on World No Tobacco Day, May 31, 2010, is no exception. The campaign is focused principally on young women—whom the National Women's Health Network claims are being increasingly targeted by tobacco companies—even though women make up only 20 percent of smokers worldwide. Posters that help to highlight the message of the campaign include an attractive model wearing a voice box with the slogan: "Chic? No, throat cancer," and one featuring a seated model with a gangrenous leg.

Former Calvin Klein model Christy Turlington is the high-profile face of this campaign. Her interest stems from having been diagnosed with early-stage emphysema following more than a decade of smoking—she started the habit at the age of 13. Her father died of lung cancer, as do more than 150,000 people in the United States annually. Turlington recorded a 30-second TV slot for the CDC that recounts the story of her father and talks about the addictive nature of nicotine and her own struggle to quit smoking.

These, then, are the five approaches we studied in order to get a handle on what components might be included in a successful retirement readiness campaign.

What appeared to be the case is that each of these campaigns falls—roughly speaking—along a continuum. At one end of the continuum are contexts, the contextual factors that act as continual reminders, provoking top-of-mind awareness for the behavior change sought; at the other end are beliefs.

We know that new habits do not get embedded overnight. Therefore these carrot-and-stick endeavors—such as additional trash cans in public places and the development of recycling initiatives for the littering and pollution issue and legislation requiring seat belts in every car plus fines for not wearing them—act as reminders until the new behavior becomes (at least in most cases) second nature.

The need for contextual factors, generally speaking, never goes away, except in the case of behaviors directly related to a discrete effort, such as the wartime campaign of Rosie the Riveter. As new populations join the pool of people from whom the desired behavior is required, anti-smoking and messages about buckling up when driving a car need to be ongoing.

As we said previously, at the other end of this continuum from context are beliefs.

Where a topic such as retirement readiness falls on this continuum depends on the optimal balance between context and beliefs. We will take the two extremes to show how this pans out. What follows is more "rule of thumb" than exact science. Obviously both context and beliefs play a role in any successful behavior change campaign, but the two intersect by different degrees.

For example, wearing seat belts is a largely contextual issue. In the years directly after 1968, when the U.S. National Highway Safety Bureau first required automobile manufacturers to install lap belts for all seats and shoulder belts for front seats, usage was thought to have been between 10 and 15 percent. Most states followed that by enacting legislation that enforced fines for failure to comply. Even though the amount of these fines is small (averaging $25 in most cases), there is something about being stopped by a traffic cop and issued a ticket that tends to keep most people in line.

Since the Click It or Ticket campaign began, seat belt usage nationally has increased from 69 percent in 1998 to around 88 percent today. As with anything aimed at influencing behavior, the likelihood of achieving 100 percent success is unrealistic. Those less likely to buckle up include commercial and pick-up truck drivers, men driving in rural areas, and people driving at night. This suggests that some people resist adhering to seat belt laws when they think they won't be seen and hence caught, while others find it inconvenient. Other groups with the tendency to buckle up least are teenagers and drivers who have been drinking; there are always some sections of the community who will throw caution to the wind!

As is the case with seat belts, when you are able to legislate to this extent you don't have to solve for much else. But in a country like America, with a Constitution that secures freedom of expression and choice in matters like retirement, we are unlikely to see legislation that would mandate U.S. citizens to save for their retirement years. The chances of a simple mandate of an initial deferral rate of, say, 6 percent, and annual auto-escalations of 2 percent until a certain desired percentage is reached—whether that be 12 percent as in Australia or 20 percent as some industry experts in the United States have found to be the upper level that consumers will bear—are slim to none. Plus, we are unlikely to see legislation that prevents employees from accessing their retirement savings until they have reached retirement age.

Of course, we already have a system in place like that, given that Social Security is a mandatory savings program where the money paid in is pooled and not available as a loan prior to the individual being eligible for benefits. But the question remains as to whether we need to protect people from themselves and make it impossible for them to draw from their retirement savings prematurely so that their long-term futures are more secure.

So, the more we are willing or able to legislate and influence behavior through contextual factors, by which people must obey or be fined heavily or punished by some other means, the less we have to appeal to the emotions as an alternative means of changing people's beliefs.

Even in wartime—the circumstances that provoked the Rosie the Riveter campaign—you can't force people to go to work. No American expected policymakers, in 1942 after the United States entered World War II, to mandate that their wife, mother, sister, or daughter had to join the war effort by getting a factory or assembly line job.

In cases such as this, where legislation is not an option, a successful public service campaign had to appeal more to people's beliefs, including—where relevant—their sense of patriotism.

The National Forest Service, on the other hand, enforces some pretty heavy fines for anyone found lighting campfires during declared fire bans. Plus, they frequently issue monetary rewards for information leading to the arrest and conviction of anyone who thoughtlessly causes a wildfire. Having said that, the environment that the National Forest Service has to police is vast, meaning that they cannot rely entirely on the punitive element. Which is where an icon like Smokey Bear comes in, to appeal to the better judgment of the general public as it relates to pro-social behavior: don't light matches or otherwise start fires in circumstances that could prove dangerous!

In the case of Smoking Is Ugly, the campaign's emphasis is concerned with the self-concept and self-esteem of young women and their beliefs around how smoking cigarettes minimizes their appeal. Additionally, it educates them about the fact that "lung cancer kills more women than breast, ovarian, and uterine cancers combined."

The campaign that falls more in the middle of this continuum of context and beliefs was the Keep America Beautiful campaign. There was an element of patriotism involved, also bolstered by efforts running prior and concurrently—such as Lady Bird Johnson's High-way Beautification Act of 1965—but it was also necessary to support these efforts with contextual factors such as the increased numbers of trash cans in public areas.

The Power of Beliefs

Historically, the financial services industry has focused largely on the belief side of the continuum, with early efforts involved at convincing individuals to save. When our focus on changing beliefs didn't arrive at the desired outcome, the pendulum swung too far in the other direction, to context. The vast majority of conversations going on in our industry right now are concerned with context: from our focus on auto-enrollment to target date investment solutions.

If we are to take a leaf out of the books of these successful public awareness campaigns, we need to design a national retirement readiness initiative that doesn't just rely on context, but also taps into the power of our beliefs at a societal as well as an individual level. This is something we don't think we have tackled well in the past and seem to be overlooking currently.

As we pointed out in the Introduction, we believe the social climate is ripe to galvanize the country around this issue. But we need a campaign with a vision—one that is specific about the behavior change we need in order for more Americans to be financially secure when they are no longer working. We need to be able to tell people what they need to *do* in simple, unambiguous terms. And that requires a clear and compelling message and perhaps an empathetic messenger, in the vein of Rosie, Smokey Bear, and the Crying Indian. Plus, we need to leverage the media so that the message reaches a wide audience frequently enough to be memorable.

Not least, we need to believe that people do have the capacity to change, given the support of contextual factors that remind them continually that they are forming new habits—which takes time and is not an overnight quick fix.

These themes, then—of context, beliefs, and resolve, and ways to tell a more compelling story rather than relying on left-brained focused statistics and factual information—are the ones we will be exploring in more depth in the following three chapters, as they relate to the issue of retirement. From a context-heavy approach we are envisioning a much more innovative, national public-will campaign that takes all of these components into account, but perhaps more than anything lays greater stress on the beliefs and emotions that all successful marketing campaigns tap into, but which our industry and government has largely ignored when it comes to talking about retirement.

First, however, let's take a look at the importance of context—the topic of the next chapter.

Chapter 7

The Power of Context

If you want to know why someone does or doesn't buy, you have to understand how the environment shapes behavior. Divorcing the quest for understanding from the context in which it takes place is a recipe for leading yourself astray.

—Philip Graves, author, *Consumerology*

In mid-September 2010, the British Broadcasting Corporation (BBC) aired the first episode in the UK of a short documentary series entitled *The Young Ones*. Its stars were anything but young. Six elderly celebrities (average age: 80 years) were to live together for a week to recreate an experiment that Harvard psychologist Professor Ellen Langer had originally devised and run in 1981. That landmark study had spawned a book by Langer with the title *Counterclockwise: Mindful Health and the Power of Possibility*. Now, almost 30 years later, viewers could watch the unfolding of another innovative counterclockwise experiment. But instead of being conducted privately with nursing home residents it was to be broadcast publicly with the aim of showing how—in just one week—it is possible for folks who consider themselves to be "over the hill" to *think* themselves young again.

The house that character actress Liz Smith and 1950s screen star Sylvia Syms would share with former TV presenter Lionel Blair, newspaper editor Derek Jameson, BBC Television's first-ever newscaster Kenneth Kendall, and international cricket umpire Dickie Bird was anything but ordinary, by today's standards at least. The country retreat had been decked out as a 1975 time capsule with suitably gaudy wallpaper, shag-pile carpets, plus kitchen appliances, furniture, and even bedding reminiscent of that particular year. Indeed, 1975 had been selected carefully as it was one in which each of these former celebrities had experienced a heyday.

But it wasn't just the house that had been given a historic make-over. The celebrities were to dress as they had in the mid-1970s: TV shows of the era were streamed into the authentic 1970s television set, and reading material would include newspapers dated 35 years earlier.

Each of the six inhabitants was being primed to remember and potentially reenact how they had thought, felt, and behaved as their younger selves by placing them in an environment that helped them do so.

In short, Langer was about to demonstrate—as she had repeatedly with other studies over the years—that the context in which we find ourselves can have a profound effect on our beliefs, behavior, and even our mental and physical well-being.

In the very first episode of this documentary series, viewers watched as 80-year-old Derek Jameson struggled to carry his own suitcase up the 14 stairs to his 1975-replica bedroom. It took him all of two minutes. Puffing and muttering to himself, he had called out for help without anyone coming to his rescue. Greeted by the BBC's "man of science" and series co-presenter, Dr. Michael Moseley, Jameson grumbled that he had told them that he couldn't climb the stairs unaided but "no one had paid a blind bit of notice." To which Moseley replied, "You didn't believe that you could, but you did."

Similarly, the eldest of the six celebrity volunteers—Liz Smith—didn't believe she could pick up a brush and paint watercolors as she had done when she was younger, but by the end of the week she was painting with gusto. Kenneth Kendall had repeatedly argued that he was much too old at 85 to even think about looking after dogs again—something which had given him much joy as a younger man—but by the end of the three-episode series he had decided to adopt a pair of King Charles' spaniels.

The other four celebrities also achieved remarkable turnarounds, physically and psychologically. In fact, when the test results of their physical abilities, dexterity, mental acuity, and even IQ were compared with those taken at the beginning of the week, the numbers were astonishing. They showed bodies that were stronger and minds that were sharper. Which, for Derek Jameson, culminated in his being able to put on his own socks for the first time in years, as well as motivating him to offer his services as a guest lecturer for young, up-and-coming journalists.

However, the producers of *The Young Ones* might have asked themselves, midway through the experiment, if they hadn't risked reversing early gains by turning their newly independent elderly volunteers into couch potatoes once again by introducing a group of professional helpers to the household. And it is here that this short series provides a cautionary note when it comes to the context-focused, auto-everything argument proposed by many people in the retirement services industry. We must balance our desire to shape behavior through contextual drivers against the potential erosion of personal responsibility, knowledge, and ability that impact our beliefs.

When their caregivers did everything for them, the inhabitants began to revert back to their old ways (figuratively and literally). They now had someone else to go upstairs for whatever it was they had forgotten, or to make that cup of tea, or to help them get dressed. The celebrity volunteers' minds and bodies adapted accordingly and they became lazier and less willing to try new things as a result. The production staff and Langer quickly saw the negative effects that this help was having on the elderly residents and so the services of these caregivers were removed.

Certainly, context counts. Undoubtedly immersing them in a 1975 environment provoked the six celebrities featured in *The Young Ones* documentary to think, feel, and act much younger than their years. But the contextual factors proved even more complex than that. The Langer study also demonstrated how inextricably connected beliefs and context really are and how by modifying either of them, the other will be affected. Even if it was a temporary and imaginary scenario, by enabling these celebrity volunteers to revisit a time when they were *not* being bombarded by social norms (beliefs) that expected older people to be frail, lose their memories, and be dependent on others, they regained much of their earlier strength, vigor, and mental sharpness.

The Context of Littering

The Keep America Beautiful (KAB) campaign discovered that context is important when it comes to dealing with the issue of littering, so they positioned trash cans to make it more convenient for people to dispose of litter and promoted fines that acted as cautionary reminders to do so. Of course, social norms and beliefs also played roles in the overall outcome.

In the summer of 2008, the KAB campaign administered a series of activities that included observing almost 10,000 people across 130 different locations in 10 states. They conducted intercept interviews with a number of these people and followed those up with a national telephone survey in order to get a better handle on who litters, why they litter, and the relative importance of contextual and individual drivers for littering behavior.

Back in 1969, when KAB published a similar study, there was only a moderate level of concern about littering; it was only starting to creep into our social conscience that this was unacceptable behavior. Today's social norms place greater emphasis on not littering and KAB's 2009 report went on to say: "Americans view litter as a serious issue; many individuals feel a personal obligation not to litter; and they want to live in clean, litter-free communities."

While littering behavior has by no means been completely elim-inated, the 2009 KAB study reported that over the intervening 40 years between that and the previous review, visible litter had decreased by some 61 percent.

Pertinent to our argument about the merits of context and beliefs, by using some pretty advanced statistical methodologies, KAB dis-covered that only about 15 percent of littering behavior could be directly accounted for by contextual variables, such as whether or not there were any trash cans in the vicinity and how far people had to walk to reach them. The majority of the variance—some 85 percent— was attributed to individual behaviors driven by personal beliefs, including a lack of motivation.

Here again, we find a distinct similarity between the littering issue and retirement readiness: people recognize that both have serious consequences, they admit to feeling a personal obligation to do something about them, and they want things to be better (to live in clean, litter-free communities; to ensure their money outlasts them, not the other way around). In both cases the context in which we find ourselves is a powerful driver of behavior, but in neither case is the problem solved by context alone.

Beliefs will always play a critical role in driving consistent behavioral change.

The retirement services industry, having spent the past 30-odd years focusing on trying to change savings behavior through educational offerings that are part of workplace retirement plans, has recognized that more needs to be done to effectively drive results. Historical efforts to drive plan participation rates, annual salary deferral rates, and appropriate participant investing have been centered on onsite meetings with employees. There has also been a considerable amount of content geared toward motivating people to save for retirement and to teach them the basics of investing.

In the past few years, especially, there has been growing recognition that these educational efforts, in and of themselves, will not solve the retirement savings crisis and that other tactics need to be employed to change behavior.

The industry has begun to shift its focus to changing the context in the workplace with powerful plan design elements in order to promote higher levels of savings. We believe there is significant merit in the discussion and use of these drivers and will explore them below, but we would be remiss in not first revisiting our cautionary note about one of the findings in *The Young Ones*: how doing too much for people tends to make them complacent. The ultimate solution to promoting true retirement readiness will have to strike a balance between contextual drivers and individual beliefs.

We are just starting to scratch the surface in understanding the power of context as it relates to voluntary saving for retirement in the workplace. It is important to note that the workplace is a considerably more controlled environment than that of our everyday lives, where littering behavior occurs. As such, we believe our ability to shape savings behavior by controlling context in the workplace is significantly more powerful than the littering example and is likely responsible for more than 15 percent of the outcome, as was the case in the 2009 KAB study.

In *Save More Tomorrow: Practical Behavioral Finance Solutions to Improve 401(k) Plans*, a publication of the Allianz Global Investors Center for Behavioral Finance, author Shlomo Benartzi demonstrates that changing the context within which people make decisions—choice architecture—can have a profound effect on the choices they make. Benartzi is a professor at the UCLA Anderson School of Management and also serves as the Chief Behavioral Economist for the Center for Behavioral Finance. In this book, Benartzi shows how proven behavioral finance techniques can be used to improve company retirement savings plans. He does an excellent job of outlining how choices and information put in the right context can powerfully promote retirement readiness across the United States.

Benartzi presents a set of ambitious goals that can be achieved in retirement plans. The goals are summarized as "90–10–90." The first "90" refers to the percentage of employees who should be participating in a voluntary retirement plan, such as a 401(k). The "10" is the goal for the percentage of annual pay that plan participants should be saving, and it's the minimum. And the final "90" is the percentage of participants who should use a one-stop, professionally managed investment (like a target date solution) for their retirement savings accounts.

You can also think of 90–10–90 as three benchmarks. As a point of reference, the equivalent statistics for the average plan are 77–06–36. If your plan hugs the averages, *Save More Tomorrow* has 20 action items that will help it meet and exceed those benchmarks. Some of those action items, such as automatic enrollment and automatic escalation, are discussed later in this chapter.

But consider this: In order to benefit from this model, you must first work for a company where you are covered by a plan. Not everyone is. Further, if the median employee tenure is just shy of five years, what happens when you change jobs or retire? Do you roll your balance over to your next employer plan or an IRA? Or do you buy that sports car you have your eye on? And if you retire having amassed a significant sum, how do you ensure it will outlast you and your spouse (if married)? How, then, might we broaden the model to address these additional important questions?

Retirement Industry Success Metrics

The model on the following page, Figure 7.1, has been expanded to contemplate these questions through three additional concepts; coverage, leakage, and longevity. Broadening the model in this way allows it to address employee access to a workplace retirement plan (coverage), to employee participation behavior (90–10–90), keeping assets in the retirement system (leakage), and the risk that a retiree will outlive their saving's ability to provide income for their lifetime (longevity).

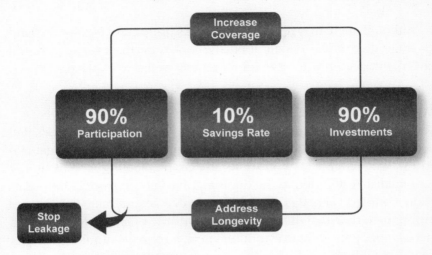

FIGURE 7.1   Plan Success Goals

Coverage

We would be remiss in discussing the concept of contextual drivers without addressing coverage, since this is the most elementary contextual driver of all. The presence of a company retirement plan for an employee is analogous to the presence of a trash can when you need one. Without a plan, employees cannot save in the workplace. Sadly, in 2010 approximately 40 percent of full-time American workers were not covered (DOL Current Population Survey 2010). When we asked what percentage of our population should be covered by a workplace retirement plan, Mark Iwry, Senior Advisor to the Secretary of the Treasury responded:

> *Coverage by workplace retirement plans should be as broad as possible, consistent with our voluntary employer-based system. To that end, under the proposed automatic IRA legislation, employers unwilling to sponsor a retirement plan would make it easy for employees to save by automatically enrolling them in workplace IRAs; employees would be free to opt out. But instead of pursuing this breakthrough in retirement savings coverage, our current*

system leaves tens of millions of working families behind; their option is to save in standalone (non-workplace) IRAs without payroll deduction or automatic enrollment, and consequently with typical take rates in the single-digit percentages.

Although there may need to be more debate around *how* we expand coverage, there is little debate about the contention that everyone should have the opportunity to save for retirement in the workplace.

Automatic Plan Features

While our discussion around using context to drive these metrics will be focused on a set of design features we term Automatic Plan Features (APFs), we recognize that in some cases implementing APFs is simply not practical, often due to the demographics of the participant population coupled with the current regulatory requirements. It is also important to note that these features are not the only way to drive plan success and, if they are truly not practical, a sponsor should find other means by which to do so. For a more comprehensive discussion about additional plan success drivers, we suggest reading *Save More Tomorrow.*

The reason we are primarily focused on these automatic plan features is because they are the clearest example of how context truly does drive behavior. So what are they and how to they work?

The Pension Protection Act of 2006 (PPA) expanded these plan design features and kicked off a significant trend in the design of voluntary workplace retirement plans. In essence, they help to shape the context of plans by taking advantage of the significant inertia demonstrated by participants in order to drive behavior. Inertia refers to the well-documented fact that if you create a default behavior in a voluntary workplace retirement plan, the vast majority of your participant base will remain in that default pattern in perpetuity.

There are three primary automatic plan features that have powerfully impacted savings behavior within the workplace in the past few years:

1. Automatic Enrollment.
2. Automatic Escalation.
3. Default to a Qualified Default Investment Alternative (QDIA).

While readers within the retirement services industry may already know this material, and the mainstream reader may not desire this amount of detail, our intent here is to draw attention to the effectiveness of these contextually sound retirement plan features, while emphasizing the need to apply them carefully. Incorrectly applied, their inherent flaws can detrimentally impact our chances of achieving retirement readiness.

The first of these features is automatic enrollment that, while seen by most practitioners as a relatively new phenomenon, has actually been around for many years. When McDonald's Corporation began its plan back in 1984 and included auto-enrollment in the plan design, it was the first company to do so. According to *Institutional Investor* magazine, at its height the plan boasted participation rates in the low 90 percent range, rates that were unheard of in the fast food industry and in fact are rare in any industry.

Ironically, McDonald's discontinued auto-enrollment in 2002—just four years before the Pension Protection Act was passed in 2006. While it had been very successful in garnering participation, the fast food industry is deemed to be less than ideal for this feature since high turnover rates often result in low account balances, abandoned accounts, and a great deal of work and cost for the plan administrators. There were concerns that McDonald's' abandonment of auto-enrollment, when the rest of the industry was contemplating further formalizing this feature, might negatively impact the future appeal of this approach. Yet these concerns turned out to be unfounded and, with the clarity provided by the PPA in 2006, other companies began adopting it. McDonald's went on to reinstate auto-enrollment in 2005, but only for its managers who likely represented a less transient workforce, thereby avoiding some of the pitfalls outlined above.

In order to understand the power of auto-enrollment, let us examine more of this feature and how it operates. Essentially, instead of requiring employees to make a proactive decision to enroll in their retirement plan, auto-enrollment does exactly the opposite. It assumes that an employee wants to enter the plan and makes the default decision that the employee is participating. So, as an employee in a plan that has auto-enrollment, you are automatically saving in the plan unless you opt out. The objective is to take advantage of employee inertia, which means that employees who are defaulted into the plan tend to remain there.

Does auto-enrollment work? It most certainly does. Opt-out rates for those who are defaulted into their retirement plans are less than 5 percent, according to a July 7, 2011, article written by David Wray of Plan Sponsor Council of America (PSCA). Also, as a point of reference, again according to PSCA, almost 42 percent of plans have an automatic enrollment feature.

There remains some controversy over the use of auto-enrollment, the criticism being that some employees are saving less money than otherwise might be the case if they were to voluntarily enroll.

The main problem, however, lies in the fact that, according to the Profit Sharing Council of America (PSCA), a staggering 74 percent of plans with automatic enrollment default participants to 3 percent or less, which is simply not enough. The Profit Sharing Council found that approximately 62 percent of plans that auto-enroll use 3 percent as a default rate. Why? While the PPA allows for higher employee deferral rates under auto-enrollment, perhaps employers are reluctant to set them higher for fear of employee complaints, driving up opt-out rates, and possibly increasing the cost of the plan itself. Only a minority (26 percent) set the default rate at 4 percent and above.

During our interviews, Catherine Collinson, President of the Transamerica Center for Retirement Studies, provided insight on a couple of key issues around auto-enrollment:

> *If you look at who auto-enrollment is going to pull into a plan, it's most likely the lower income employees. So what are you doing? You're pulling that person in at 3 percent. That's a moral hazard because it is implying that saving 3 percent is enough, which it most certainly is not. It's also pulling them in at 3 percent without adequate messaging about the Saver's Credit, which approximately three out of four people are likely to miss because they don't know about it.*

While 3 percent may seem like the wrong answer today, can you imagine trying to break ground on this idea? Coincidentally, Mark Iwry was present at the groundbreaking and shares his story about how 3 percent became the go-to default rate.

In 1998 when I was at Treasury in a previous incarnation, we decided to define something called automatic enrollment, describe and approve it under the 401(k) rules, and then actually promote it. We issued a ruling with a 3 percent auto-enrollment level for initial contributions as an illustration of the idea. It caught on pretty slowly. In fact as I tried to encourage the private sector to do it—other than the few who had been doing it previously with some hesitations because they didn't know if it was legal or not—not a whole lot more joined in. The industry was not supportive . . . generally there was indifference, lukewarm support at best; mild opposition was probably the dominant reaction."

That's right: the 3 percent default rate that is so commonly used today is the result of *an illustration*, not something that was meant to be accepted as a recommendation, yet that's precisely what happened.

Our contention is that auto-enrollment has taught us a great deal about participant behavior and has successfully accomplished what we have asked of it. Now we just need to change what it is we are asking for. The current situation with auto-enrollment is that it is ensuring more employees enroll in their plans but at a deferral rate that is far too low to move the needle with respect to retirement readiness. The answer seems so simple—just increase the auto-enrollment default rate and the results will improve. And, indeed, there is building evidence that increasing the default rate beyond 3 percent does not have the previously anticipated negative impact of increasing opt-out rates. In fact, it seems to have very little impact at all. In a July 15, 2011, release titled, *Fidelity Thought Leadership: Auto-Enrollment and WSJ Article: The Rest of the Story*, Fidelity shared their experience that "roughly 90 percent of AE eligible parts do not opt out—regardless of how high the default deferral rate is." [Note: "AE is an abbreviation for auto-enrollment and "parts" for participants.]

The Power of Auto-Escalation

Let's now leave automatic enrollment aside and turn to the second contextual plan design feature: automatic escalation.

Essentially, auto-escalation builds on the initial deferral percentage selected by the employee or established by the employer in an auto-enrollment plan. For example, if the employee begins at 3 percent, auto-escalation will increase it from there. This too can be a powerful force, because it also takes advantage of behavioral inertia to increase participant deferral rates automatically throughout their tenure.

According to the PSCA, auto-escalation is present in just under 38 percent of auto-enrollment plans, which means that the combination of auto-enrollment and auto-escalation, which is critical to creating a context conducive to a fully funded retirement, is only present in about 16 percent of plans. And, of all plans with automatic escalation, the majority (57 percent) cap it at 6 percent of pay or below.

Since the amount an employee defers into their retirement plan is among the most important determinants of ultimate retirement readiness, let us sum up these automatic features and what the average auto-enrollment plan might be expected to yield.

As outlined above, 42 percent of plans automatically enroll employees. Seventy-three percent of these use a default deferral rate of 3 percent or less and only 38 percent of them use an auto-escalation feature, with the most common cap being 6 percent. Keeping in mind that the median tenure of an employee is approximately five years, this is how it will likely play out.

Imagine you are a participant in the average auto-everything plan. You will likely be enrolled at 3 percent and remain there until you terminate your employment, since auto-escalation is currently the exception rather than the rule. If you are lucky enough to work for a company with the foresight to include auto-escalation, then your 3 percent might be escalated 1 percent each year for the next four years when, at least according to the statistics, you are most likely to end your employment with that company. Roughly calculated, your average contribution to that plan would be 5 percent. At these levels, whether you have auto-escalation or not, your auto-enrollment plan is not designed to provide you with enough money for a secure retirement. Although, should you choose to do so, you could always increase the level of your contributions.

How might the above numbers change if we were to get a bit more aggressive? Let's use the example of an auto-enrollment rate of 6 percent, with 2 percent annual escalations, and a cap of 12 percent. Over that same five-year tenure, your contribution would double, averaging close to 10 percent, which is a much more reasonable track to a retirement ready future.

Qualified Default Investment Alternative

Having reviewed auto-enrollment and auto-escalation, let us now turn to the third automatic enrollment feature: the defaulting of investments into a Qualified Default Investment Alternative (QDIA).

If the amount an employee defers into their plan is the number one driver of retirement readiness, another very important factor is how that employee invests. As we have outlined throughout this book, the vast majority of people struggle to know how to best invest their own retirement accounts.

Again, some helpful news came with the Pension Protection Act. It established the concept of the QDIA that, simply stated, says an employer can default a participant into an appropriate investment without the risk of being sued, provided that certain qualifications are met. The relief from liability became available under Section 404(c) of ERISA (the previously mentioned 1974 landmark legislation). Prior to the Pension Protection Act, Section 404(c) relief was only available when a participant selected their own investments.

This new development provided an important tool for the industry to begin more aggressively defaulting employees into the kind of appropriate investments that they would be less likely to select on their own. In addition, it provided relief for plan sponsors who offered auto-enrollment in their plan and used a QDIA as the destination for defaulted employee deferrals. QDIAs generally take the form of a fund or solution with a balanced combination of investments such as stocks, bonds, and cash, and consider both age and risk tolerance. These investments are often referred to as balanced, target date, or lifecycle solutions and they have gained in popularity as a result of the advent of the QDIA. For example, according to EBRI/ICI 2010, usage of target date solutions among recently hired employees has jumped from 28.3 percent in 2006 to 47.6 percent in 2010.

These three automatic plan features—auto-enrollment, auto-escalation, and QDIA—have proven to be powerful contextual drivers of savings behavior. With just a small adjustment to the rates at which we auto-enroll and auto-escalate, we could have a dramatic impact on retirement savings rates in the workplace.

But let us not forget that we live in a messy, complex world in which the unexpected often happens. Which brings us to our next topic: the leakage of savings from existing plans.

Leakage

We know that the earlier you begin saving the easier it is to secure your retirement and that the ability to commit to saving over an extended period of time, uninterrupted, is critical to outcome. That's the ideal scenario.

What is less than ideal is what is known as *leakage*. In the retirement system, this comes in the form of employee loans, hardship withdrawals, and balances that are not rolled over when an employee changes jobs. Each of these challenges means that considerable assets are effectively leaving an already underfunded retirement system. In order for us to successfully increase retirement readiness, we not only have to increase savings, we also have to minimize this leakage. But how?

In the 112th Congress, bills were introduced in both the House and the Senate to help reduce leakage from the defined contribution retirement system. The SEAL Act—Savings Enhancement by Alleviating Leakage in 401(k) Savings Act of 2011—proposed key changes designed to keep retirement savings in the system, including:

◆ The extension of the rollover period for participant loans in the event an employee loses his or her job. Typically, outstanding loan balances are due upon separation from service and if not paid back, taxes and tax penalties are due.

◆ The ability for 401(k) participants to make contributions to their plan during the six months following a hardship withdrawal. Current law prohibits participant contributions during this period.

◆ And, the outlawing of the 401(k) debit cards which encourage participants to treat their accounts like temporary savings.

While these proposed changes cannot, in and of themselves, eliminate leakage from the retirement system, they do represent the kind of thinking necessary to make an impact. In addition, employers and industry need to design plans with leakage in mind. Simple examples like limiting loans to one per participant (which was also originally in the SEAL Act), or setting defaults to roll assets to an IRA upon separation from a company, may meaningfully reduce leakage and need to be explored.

Another challenge we need to take into account concerns the length of time a plan participant might live, beyond the average established by actuarial studies.

Longevity

Up to this point we have discussed the contextual factors involved in driving savings and investing behavior while employees are working, collecting a paycheck, and accumulating assets for retirement. But what happens when an employee retires and needs to ensure their savings will last for a lifetime, especially when the length of that life cannot be predicted? The challenge of making one's money last is commonly referred to as *longevity risk*. Ironically the one thing we all desire—to live a long life—can also represent our biggest challenge in financial terms. The fact is most of us will either outlive, or fail to reach, our life expectancy, and often by more than just a few years. So what happens if we plan on living to 86, yet end up living to 100, or even 104?

As previously discussed, because many defined benefit plans promised payments for a lifetime, they also helped to mitigate this risk of outliving one's income. Defined contribution plans, on the other hand, do not. This difference between the two has become increasingly important with the trend toward DC plans and away from traditional DB plans. In a recent report released by the Executive Office of the President—Council of Economic Advisors, the challenge is summarized as follows:

> *In 1980, 71 percent of private employer-sponsored retirement plan assets were held in DB plans (including cash balance plans), but by 2009, 60 percent of these assets were held in DC plans. While 401(k)-type plans offer workers some important advantages—such as portability, high potential for growth, and flexibility—the shift to 401(k)-type plans also has transferred substantial risk from employers to workers. The aggregate shift from traditional DB plans to 401(k)-type plans and hybrid DB plans highlights the problem of diminished prevalence of lifetime income benefits. This trend is exacerbated by lump-sum payouts from defined benefit plans. One study found that, among those offered the choice in a traditional DB plan, 73 percent elected to take a lump sum (Mottola and Utkus 2007).*

The report goes on to discuss the benefits of annuities and how, "Annuities can help to mitigate some of the risk faced by retirees. In particular, annuities protect retirees against the risk of outliving assets." It then introduces the term, the *Annuity Puzzle*, which means that in spite of their risk-mitigating properties, for a myriad of reasons annuities are simply not being used in a meaningful way by retirees. The report ends with recommendations for "Removing Barriers to Annuitization" "by easing and simplifying regulations that have limited lifetime income." For those interested in further exploration of this topic, there is significant activity around the concept of lifetime income and consequently a plethora of information available. A good starting point might be the report referenced earlier.

While annuities may represent a partial solution to the challenge of longevity, they are likely only part of the answer that will emerge as a result of the current focus on this very serious issue.

To summarize our aspiration: a new vision for retirement readiness has to begin with coverage in order to ensure that every American worker has the ability to save in a workplace retirement plan. We then turn to behavior within the plan itself and look to Professor Benartzi's model (90–10–90): 90 percent participation in the plan; contributions at 10 percent of pay; and 90 percent invested in a fully managed solution. Additionally, the industry must work to limit leakage from plans to ensure assets remain committed to retirement savings, and retirees need to be aware of longevity risk and be exposed to solutions for income that cannot be outlived.

But let us now revisit the work around litter in America by KAB and the BBC's *The Young Ones* study. While context is a powerful driver of behavior, people's beliefs are indeed needed to bring about sustained change. When the helpers were brought in to assist the celebrity volunteers in the *The Young Ones* program, that simple, well-meaning change of context resulted in retrograde behavior. Similarly, if we know that the median employee tenure is approximately five years, during which time employees may have been defaulted into plans with no need for them to think personally about their retirement; then what happens when they change jobs? The context has changed but, without the necessary belief around saving for their retirement, what are the odds that all of these employees will keep their savings intact and continue a pro-saving behavior?

Context varies over time, as we have pointed out before: we marry, take on more debt, have children, change jobs—all of these are an inherent part of life in addition to the increasing churn and flexibility exhibited in today's workplace. While automatic plan features help bring more people into the system, they do not necessarily inculcate in them good savings habits. For that, we have to turn back to beliefs which, in relation to retirement readiness, means helping Americans see the advantages of taking responsibility for their own lives and fostering in them the resolve to sustain those beliefs until they become habitual.

Beliefs are the focus of the next chapter.

Chapter 8

Beliefs and Resolve

The best time to plant a tree was 20 years ago. The second best time is today.

—Chinese proverb

I t was the first and only time in his 32 years as a financial advisor that John Mott had experienced anything like it.

Typically, his enrollment meetings or monthly reviews would go something like this: A company would ask him to fly in on a Sunday evening in order to prepare for all-day meetings with their employees the next day. On this particular occasion some 250 employees at one location had been told that Mott was available to meet with them one-on-one to discuss the company's 401(k) plan. The company had freed up each employee for 30 minutes because, with participation currently low—at around 40 percent—the plan sponsors realized that this informational event was sorely needed to make the advantages of saving for retirement more widely understood and accepted. Those individual meetings were to be followed up with a companywide get-together at a nearby theater the next day. To attend the Tuesday event all an employee had to do was to collect an explanatory postcard and sign up.

Monday arrived. John saw four people for his one-on-ones—out of a potential 150 employees who were not yet participating in the 401(k) plan. His day was over by 10:30 a.m. Only one of those individuals actually wanted to talk about retirement. The rest used the opportunity to ask general questions, since it was the first time they had ever sat down with a financial services expert. One woman wanted to know how she could get her two grown sons who still lived with her to start paying rent.

Tuesday came and things were not much better. Only eight employees showed up at the theater, all young men who had been told by their parents that they needed to find out more about their company's pension plan.

Ask any of those who have ever tried to engage employees during these enrollment meetings and they will tell you that oftentimes people come just because there is free food.

Ask John Mott why he thinks so few people are interested to learn about the advantages of saving money for their retirement, especially those who are closest to reaching that point in their lives, and he says, "You know, it's interesting. The older generation, if they're not in the plan, they're not getting into one. They think it's too late. And I don't know how you change those beliefs."

Yet that was not an issue at a different company John told us about, an experience that has stuck in his memory ever since because of its uniqueness:

> *The president of this company took it upon himself to get as many of his employees into the plan as he could. So, before our meetings he would stand up and his message was, "You know what? I hired you because I thought you were smart and if you're not in this plan then you're not that smart," and everybody got in because he was the president with the ability to hire and fire.*

> *Call it what you will, but we almost got up to 100 percent participation during those series of meetings, just because of what he said, the bottom line of which was "you guys are idiots if you're not in this plan, and I didn't hire idiots."*

There is a chasm a mile wide between those two forms of leadership, both with regards to their belief in the importance of retirement savings and their resolve in ensuring that each employee takes advantage of what is being offered. But, as with our earlier discussion around auto-everything, and the learning from Ellen Langer's *Counterclockwise* research on what happens when decision-making responsibility is taken away from individuals, there may still be some downside to the approach of that well-meaning president, although not as much as with plan sponsors who take a more relaxed attitude around plan participation.

Retirement savings does not constitute a single event. It's not as simple as making that first good investment decision and you are done. Changing jobs, major life events such as getting married or having children, and taking on bigger financial commitments while we are still working, all impact whether or not that initial decision remains valid; usually not. Which means that what we originally opted to do around deferral rates for our retirement savings plan needs to be reassessed on a regular basis. It's one thing to have that first participation decision taken off our plates, because we know there is value in auto-enrollment. But when you combine that with the current lack of financial literacy overall, the likelihood is that the money we have saved is ultimately not going to meet our retirement needs.

The Issue of Stakeholder Resolve

Earlier, when we discussed the importance of financial literacy, we looked at retirement readiness through the lens of a lack of knowledge. In this chapter we are going to dig deeper into how this issue is impacted by resolve and beliefs. This is not just about the beliefs and resolve of individuals, but of all stakeholders—the plan sponsor (employer), industry advisors, and policymakers.

Specifically, we wanted to get a handle on whether or not we are willing—as a society and individually—to change our behavior around saving for retirement, as well as do what is needed to support that change. In short, do we have the personal resolve, corporate resolve, and political resolve to change our approach to retirement readiness in a meaningful way?

But before doing that, let us look at two topics, beliefs and resolve, and in particular the relationship between them.

If we consider John Mott's earlier hypothesis about why older employees choose not to get into a retirement plan, because they think it's too late, it's obvious that beliefs play a role in strengthening or weakening our resolve. In fact there is one type of belief that psychologists call *self-efficacy* that seems particularly relevant here.

Originally coined by Albert Bandura in his seminal paper entitled "Self-Efficacy: Toward a Unifying Theory of Behavior Change," self-efficacy refers to the beliefs we hold about what we are personally capable of doing under changing and challenging circumstances.

Self-efficacy beliefs are said to be "the most important determinants of the behaviors people choose to engage in and how much they persevere in their efforts in the face of obstacles and challenges." Self-efficacy beliefs, then, impact our resolve. These beliefs originate in childhood where we first develop the capacity to understand cause-and-effect relationships, and are modified over time as we discover the extent to which we are able to manipulate and control our external environment.

While getting a person to articulate their beliefs as they relate to savings behavior can be quite difficult, because often they are subconscious, this is clearly an area where actions speak much louder than words. Watching an individual's (or society's) behavior and what they are resolved to do provides us with a clear window into their underlying beliefs.

So with that focus in mind, let us look at the issue of resolve regarding retirement readiness for the following stakeholders.

Individual Resolve

Historically, one of the biggest fears we face as we grow older is becoming a burden on our families. Avoiding that outcome doesn't happen by accident; it has to be planned for. Where the money comes from to do that, of course, has always been a challenge for many. It is just that the challenges—or should we call them what they are, the temptations—we face today are increasing and insidious.

There are things we spend money on today that we didn't have 10 or even 5 years ago. We are no longer looking only at cable TV (figuratively and literally), but access to the Internet. It used to be just a cell phone bill but now it is iPhones, iPads, and e-readers, all of which come with data plans that nudge those bills to $1,200 a year or more. It takes considerable resolve on the part of individuals these days not to get caught up in the runaway consumerism that is now the social norm. And in stark contrast to the experience of our parents and grandparents, the era of easy access to credit means that we no longer have to save to buy what we want, we can have it today—just by putting that purchase on our credit cards.

There are plenty of alarming statistics to mull over:

◆ According to the Federal Reserve report on consumer debt released in July 2011, total U.S. revolving debt was $793.1 billion, 98 percent of which is made up of credit card debt.

◆ Those households with credit card debt carry an average outstanding balance of $15,799.

◆ The average consumer today will have 13 credit obligations on record at a credit reporting agency, 9 of which are likely to be credit cards, including department store charge cards and bank cards, plus four installment loans such as auto loans, mortgage loans, and student loans.

As we pointed out in Chapter One, Boomers may have earned more, but they have also spent more and as a consequence acquired considerably more debt than their predecessors.

But a U.S. savings rate close to zero doesn't truly shine a light on where the biggest issue lies. Former Chief Economist of the World Bank Joseph E. Stiglitz pointed this out in a *Vanity Fair* article on the economic crisis, writing, "Here's the reality: in the years leading up to the recession, according to research done by my Columbia University colleague Bruce Greenwald, the bottom 80 percent of the American population had been spending around 110 percent of its income."

How much of that were we individually spending on securing our future retirement? Precious little.

With finite resources, the more money that goes into creating debt, the less we have to fund our retirement savings. Part of our resolve, then, is to consider what that new smart phone and data plan is costing us, not just over the course of a lifetime, but in relation to the lost opportunities from failing to save sufficiently for retirement. In all honesty, how many of us ever do that math?

The contagion of consumerism in our country today is such that one of our interviewees described how, in his neighborhood, the minute one household invested in a large-scale expansion of their home, everyone else in the area followed suit.

This epic battle between consumerism and saving plays out in many ways. Because of the way we have firmly established ourselves as a spending society, organizations that are encouraging us to save are often doing so on the heels of consumerism. This engenders the feeling that we are more responsible spenders if part of that money comes back to us in some form of saving, as is often seen with cash rebate programs, some of which may even end up in our savings account. Additionally, our mailboxes (physical and electronic) are full of offers telling us that by spending over $500 on item X we can save 50 percent on item Y. It is hard not to feel overwhelmed by the sell side of our culture and misinterpret this as the only (or at least the main) way in which we can actually save money.

Unfortunately this is not a cut-and-dried issue; there is no simple solution. As Nevin Adams pointed out, with respect to his recent purchase of the latest iPhone:

> *I remember having the discussion with my wife about it. I felt bad about how much the phone itself was costing, let alone the data plans. But as she pointed out, that's part and parcel of how I work these days. Essentially, to go without it would increase my level of frustration because it would mean not being able to do all the things from my phone that I now take for granted.*

Any service-focused entrepreneur or constantly traveling salesperson or executive knows exactly how he feels. But what about when we are compelled to trade in our standard TV for the latest 3D plasma set, which cannot be justified as a necessary part of how we do work in the twenty-first century? Do we really believe that most people fully consider whether they can afford items like these, or contemplate how they are failing to invest in their future retirement as a result of their present-day spending?

Yet when it comes to our self-efficacy beliefs around retirement, a great many people that the advisors and other industry experts we spoke with encountered react to the advice to save 6 or even 10 percent of their income before tax with "I can't afford to do it." That response immediately negates any resolve to question that perspective or take any action to see if it can be contradicted. Maybe this has something to do with our tendency to believe that spending and saving are on opposite ends of a continuum and that it's a case of either/or?

Yet with some people like Amy Haley, whom we introduced in Chapter 1, there is a balance that can be struck between sensibly setting aside a certain percentage of income on a regular basis and enjoying daily treats like a breakfast burrito or decent cup of coffee.

The President of Moreton Retirement Partners, Chad Larsen, agrees that when it comes to the resolve to save, it is not an either/or argument. Yet erroneous beliefs persist among the employee groups he meets. Everyone he speaks with says they believe it is hard for them to save money. Many get upset when Larsen counters that by suggesting that saving money has nothing to do with a person's income. As he goes on to point out, we all know somebody who makes lots of money but can't seem to save a dime of it.

"If it were just about making more money those people would be greater savers, and they're not," says Larsen. "Then I explain that I've also worked with thousands of people over the years that make next to nothing who consistently save 3, 4, 5 . . . sometimes as much as 7 percent of their income. But I don't believe you're either a spender or a saver."

Then why are we not better—collectively as well as individually—at achieving a balance between enjoying life in the present while also, like Amy Haley, shoring up the freedom and security that an adequately-funded retirement plan provides?

Perhaps it's not just a question of having the resolve to live within our means, but having a better handle on what we are looking to achieve in terms of how much we need to be saving for retirement. For the vast majority of us, the workplace serves as the critical place to strike a balance for doing this. That assumes that we have access to a workplace retirement plan in the first place, however. So what beliefs and resolve are prevalent when it comes to the employer's side of this equation?

Plan Sponsor Resolve

While there are many great examples of employers who take their responsibilities very seriously, unfortunately not all of them make the long-term security of their employees a primary focus. Some lack the basic financial literacy, at least in relation to the retirement plan they are promoting, that would enable them to make good decisions on behalf of their employees. For example, one of our interviewees shared how he was talking with a group of CEOs who were responsible for running their retirement plans about adding automatic enrollment when one of them asked, "What's that?" While it is understood that not everyone knows the intricacies of plan design, a plan sponsor's understanding of the features that drive retirement readiness is critical.

The same lack of resolve that plagues participants is often experienced at the plan sponsor level. According to Nevin Adams:

> *Plan sponsors have an inertia problem and they tend to look to the middle of the pack because they've all seen the movie about what happens to the wildebeest that wanders away from the herd. They don't want to be that wildebeest. So they're all looking for the same sweet spot, the middle of the crowd, where everybody else is. And where that is, certainly after the Pension Protection Act, is to start people in at 3 percent.*

As mentioned in the previous chapter, the 3 percent Adams is referring to is the rate at which most plans with automatic enrollment default their participants into the plan—a rate that is just too low to produce a retirement-ready employee. As Adams points out, some plan sponsors are going way beyond that, with a growing number of employers willing to ratchet auto-enrollment up to the full match level and beyond. But in a tough economy that can be a challenging call to make, as some employers are already struggling with maintaining their existing contributions and other benefits.

The fact is, increasing participation levels also increases an employer's plan costs overall, so it takes considerable resolve on their part to pay more for plan expenses and potentially more for employer matching. And as several of our experts admitted, convincing an employer that increasing their employer matching contributions or attracting more employees to their plan will make it increasingly likely that they will engage better, longer-term employees, needs to be backed up by data, data that has been hard to come by.

Nevertheless, there is growing evidence to support the importance of retirement benefits to today's employees, evidence that strongly implies that an employer will be rewarded, through employee loyalty, for a stronger resolve to their employee retirement plan. For example, when employees were asked about the importance of workplace retirement benefits in the Thirteenth Annual Transamerica Center for Retirement Studies Survey, "The vast majority of workers (90%) value retirement benefits as important—61 percent say retirement plans are 'very important.'" In fact, "retirement benefits hold such great importance among workers that more than half (53%) said that they would leave their current employer for a nearly identical job with a similar employer if it offered better retirement benefits." It stands to reason that if employees would leave for better retirement benefits, they would also stay for them.

But beginning any discussion about resolve by focusing on how plan sponsors can increase participation and employee deferrals is a bit like starting a bike race on the last climb before the finish. Where this may very well be where the race is won, it most certainly isn't where the initial focus must be placed. Before we can have the discussion about participation rates in a workplace plan, we have to start by ensuring that there is a plan in which to participate in the first place. As previously discussed, there are still a great many employers who do not sponsor a retirement plan and, as a consequence, a great many employees who do not have the ability to save in the workplace. So, resolve really starts with an employer ensuring that their employees are offered this opportunity.

Until employers strengthen their resolve around their responsibility to encourage employees to save for their retirement, we will make scant progress around the issue of retirement readiness. The extent to which employers prioritize this important topic does profoundly impact the extent to which the American worker embraces it. Prioritization starts with offering a plan and continues with driving savings behavior. We need to recognize that there will likely be more cost and effort involved in doing it right, but also the one place that the average American has succeeded in saving for retirement is the workplace.

Many employees are still without a workplace retirement plan and most employers that do offer plans are not having the tough conversations to get them to participate at the appropriate rates. So, where does the responsibility for this effort lie? Perhaps it starts with less timidity and more blunt honesty from the retirement industry itself. Because, as John Mott pointed out, he's never come across another company leader willing to say what that president said about expecting the smart people he hired to also be smart about their retirement options; everyone else seems to be significantly more cautious in their approach.

Industry Resolve

Paul Henry is Managing Director, Retirement Clients and Products, at LIMRA International:

> *I have often thought that as an industry we've focused on the wrong things in terms of the dialog we have with employers about their plans. When they have a 75 percent participation rate we say, congratulations, you're doing just fine. What we rarely, if ever, talk about with these employers is how many of their employees are on track to replacing half, maybe even 60 or 70 percent, of their income in retirement. Shouldn't that be the measure of plan health?*

When considering the issue of resolve and the beliefs that support or mitigate it, much comes back to what we discussed in the State of the Union chapter: what is our goal, our vision, as an industry? If it is to get people on the path to financial security during retirement, then we need a new paradigm around what constitutes plan health. This is not a message that is well served by timidity.

There is a growing body of industry professionals who are willing to visit with plan sponsors and say, "Here's what we believe you should do with respect to your plan. You have a responsibility to manage your plan to optimize retirement readiness, which means going with a 6 percent versus 3 percent auto-enrollment plan, employing auto-escalation, or simply designing your plan for maximum participation by whatever means possible. We are emphatically saying that this is the right answer for your employees."

Are enough of these conversations going on right now? A number of our industry experts felt there were not, and perhaps the reason is that, as much as we would like it to be the case, there is no one-size-fits-all solution. But that shouldn't deflect us as industry professionals from being more forceful around where we see possibilities for improvement.

To illustrate what we mean, consider this example from former Managing Director at IBM Retirement Funds, Jay Vivian. Let's say that Company A instituted auto-enrollment and now has 90 percent participation in their pension plan; only 10 percent of employees have chosen to opt out. Compare that to Company B where the participation rate is only 60 percent. Which company do you consider to be the most successful in the pension plan stakes? You would think Company A, right?

The problem is, we know that with auto-enrollment people aren't as engaged in the plan. So we might look at these two companies in five years' time and find that the auto-enroll company still has a participation rate of 90 percent, but almost all of the employees are still only at 3 percent deferral. Whereas Company B is up to 70 percent participation but average deferral rate is up, on average, to 6 percent. From the perspective of what the overall goal is—security during retirement—company B's employees are in much better shape than company A's. But, unless we're very clear on the outcome that as an industry we are in business to bring about, we're always going to be sidetracked by the wrong numbers.

And where industry resolve is concerned, we are frequently focused on what fails to make a real difference, although to myopically focus on industry is perhaps the wrong unit of measurement here. The retirement industry, like any other, is made up of people. It is not only the degree to which industry is willing to deliver the message, but also the degree to which the individuals who make up our industry are prepared to give strong, honest guidance to plan sponsors and participants that represents the beliefs and resolve we need to change our current savings culture.

These frank individuals, whom Charlie Ruffell collectively calls the 401(k) Whisperers, are people like Paul D'Aiutolo, a plan advisor with UBS Financial Services.

Early on in his career, one of the first people D'Aiutolo sat down with during a one-on-one was a woman in her mid-sixties who worked at a nursing facility. As she got older she was finding the work harder to do, the kind of heavy lifting work that involves removing patients from their beds to sit in wheelchairs, taking them to the toilet, and changing their clothes. She was looking forward to her retirement very much, and hopefully very soon.

D'Aiutolo asked her to tell him about her lifestyle and they began going through the numbers. She would only get around $800–900 a month from Social Security because of her pay grade and the fact that she had started work later than most. Her retirement assets stood at

$23,000 total. But her expenses ran to something like $3,000 a month. D'Aiutolo explained that the best she could hope for if she retired right then, as she had expected to do, was $1,200 a month. With nothing else to her name there was no way she could make up that shortfall. She would have to keep on working.

"From my perspective I felt like I was an oncologist telling someone they had cancer and only one year to live," recalls D'Aiutolo. "We just have to do better. We have to do better as an industry to not have people in that position."

That's the passion that drives a 401(k) Whisperer. These are the people who are concerned with doing what truly moves the needle toward retirement readiness and understanding what plan participants and plan sponsors need and why. According to D'Aiutolo, as an industry we are missing the mark. Our resolve is often to sell products and services instead of solving problems, to focus on tools and features and to obsess over product differentiation, whereas we should be focused on encouraging more employees to save and invest wisely for their future.

D'Aiutolo and the many other 401(k) Whisperers we interviewed for this book know whom they are in business to serve. "My job is to solve the problems of the little guy so that they can ultimately retire someday," D'Aiutolo says. "I think that's what we in the industry have to do and largely we just don't."

Even as the retirement industry refocuses on those we are in business to serve, we need to create a compelling message around retirement readiness, one that is brand agnostic with respect to our individual desires to promote product awareness and sell business. This message cannot come from industry alone. Were that to happen we would likely be accused of being self-serving, open to the same sort of criticism leveled at the packaging manufacturers who were behind the Keep America Beautiful campaign.

We have to engage the support and backing of all stakeholders, including government. But what beliefs and resolve do we find there?

Government Resolve

Balancing short-term economic cycles with long-term economic health is undoubtedly a challenge. As we have seen and may even have come to understand, there are certain economic levers at the government's disposal to help with this endeavor. Short-term interest rates are the classic example. Given that our current economy is highly dependent on the health of the consumer and consumer spending, another economic lever comes in the form of direct consumer stimulus programs. During the latest economic downturn that began in 2008, this lever was used on two occasions, first with the Economic Stimulus Act of 2008 during the Bush Administration, when families received up to a $600 tax rebate to help spur consumer spending. The other occurred in May of 2009 as a result of the American Recovery and Reinvestment Act under the Obama Administration, where $250 checks were sent to more than 52 million Social Security recipients. While perhaps not explicitly stated, the message was clear in both cases, do your part to spur the economy—spend that money!

As Nevin Adams points out, "What are we telling people? People continue to fret about the funding status of Social Security, but when there's a here-and-now interest in encouraging spending, we declare a payroll tax holiday, hoping that people will take that 2 percent—money that would have gone toward funding Social Security retirement—and spend it. It's a message, albeit an implied one, that runs counter to the importance of retirement savings."

Paul Henry of LIMRA agrees, saying that whenever there is a stimulus tax credit, "It's never, 'Here's $600, go save it.'"

Recognizing that the purpose of these programs is indeed to stimulate the economy, it is not surprising that the message is to spend that money. But what is missing—and perplexing when you consider our government's concern with the lack of retirement readiness in this country—is an equal and opposite message to save. Any message from government to save for the future is, at best, muted when compared to the message to keep our economy healthy by spending more. The balance between these two kinds of messages needs to change if we are to make any real progress toward retirement readiness.

Nevertheless, this tug-of-war extends far beyond simple messaging. With the high U.S. government debt level, all options seem to be on the table in the attempt to close the deficit. In addition to discussions about eliminating items like the mortgage deduction on a second home, savings limits for 401(k) plans are also being discussed.

Recognizing that the task of balancing the budget is one of monumental significance, eroding the American worker's ability to save for retirement still seems incredibly shortsighted. Does not long-term thinking and a long-term solution dictate that we balance spending today with saving for tomorrow? If any changes are to be made, shouldn't they be in favor of increasing savings, not decreasing them? The bottom line is that in the long run healthy savings rates are synonymous with a healthy economy, because without them we will have far too many people without the means to contribute to their well-being and far too few with the ability to support them.

Consider, too, that during a recent Legg Mason Advisory Council meeting, a think tank set up to contemplate increasing retirement readiness, the topic of messaging came up, specifically around what minimum percentage Americans should be told to save to increase their odds of being retirement ready. Several council members felt there would be opposition were that number to be set much higher than 10 percent. While we think that this concern may be unwarranted, the simple fact that the concern came up speaks volumes.

The good news is that whereas a number of 401(k) Whisperers are present in the retirement services industry, they are also present in government. People like Mark Iwry, who bring a common sense approach to the challenge, instill confidence that progress can be made on the issue of retirement readiness. His early work on auto-enrollment is starting to bear fruit and his current work on mitigating longevity risk is likely to do the same. Also falling into this category are Senators Rob Portman (R-OH) and Ben Cardin (D-MD), who were integral to the advances in pension legislation within the Economic Growth and Tax Relief Reconciliation Act of 2001 (EGTRRA) and the Pension Protection Act of 2006 (PPA), and there are many examples just like them. What we need are more policymakers who truly appreciate the challenges we face, who are committed to retirement readiness, and are willing to boldly cross the political aisle in the name of bipartisan progress.

One of the points raised by our interviewees was that, living in a democracy, it is we, the people, who are ultimately responsible for the resolve shown by our government. After all, good representatives focus on what their constituency cares about, and every two years every member of the House of Representatives and one third of the Senate come up for reelection. It's our job to demonstrate to our representatives that retirement stability is something we deeply care about, and it's their job to represent us on topics they know to be important to us and to society overall. How they support this important topic should be included in the criteria we use in evaluating their suitability for guiding us into a secure future. What part does their perspective and focus on retirement savings play in our decision to reelect them? If not at all, maybe this is a conversation we each need to be responsible for putting back on the table.

What, Then, Is Our Message?

As far as each of our responsibilities is concerned, a good place to start would be to shift our focus on what we applaud as a society so that it is less of what we *have* in terms of material possessions and more of what we've *done* in relation to ensuring long-term financial security and stability for ourselves, our loved ones, and our country. Given the right message and messenger—actually the right *story*, which is the topic we turn to in the next chapter—that cultural shift is no more challenging than overturning the concept of the "little woman" who was thought barely strong enough to lift a roasting pan out of the oven for Sunday lunch before Rosie the Riveter burst on the scene in 1942.

In the same way that contextual factors can be put in place to boost the wearing of seat belts or to reduce littering, it appears that we need to address the contextual issues that detrimentally affect our self-efficacy beliefs and hence our resolve with respect to retirement readiness.

Perhaps what we have experienced over the past few decades has been the inevitable confusion that resulted from shifting from the defined benefit era to the defined contribution era. While not wishing to use a term as dramatic as a lost generation (or two) with respect to retirement savings, it appears that many people *have* gotten lost in the shuffle. As the popularity of defined benefit plans has waned and defined contribution plans have taken their place, many seem to have missed the message that we each need to take ownership of our retirement in much the same way that we now have to take responsibility for our careers.

But perhaps that message was too quietly and timidly expressed in the first place—so much so that it was nearly impossible to hear. That is a charge that could be leveled at all the constituents involved in this issue of retirement readiness. Maybe, too, that is where our beliefs—not just around self-efficacy but what we are capable of bearing as a nation—are failing us.

For many years psychologists have studied the subtle ways that teachers' expectations concerning the abilities of their students unwittingly affect those students' outcomes. In the classic Rosenthal-Jacobson study referred to as *Pygmalion in the Classroom*, for example, teachers were deliberately given inaccurate information about which students belonged to the top 20 percent on a particular test; the list of names in fact had been drawn up randomly. At the end of the year the students were tested again and the scores of those whose names had been on the fictitious top 20 percent list were found to be significantly higher than the rest. This was taken as evidence that, subconsciously or otherwise, "you get what you expect," and that when teachers believe that some students are brighter than others they treat them with "subtle favoritism."

Similarly, are our expectations around what the average American can withstand with respect to hearing a straightforward, honest message about retirement readiness lower than our country deserves?

We underestimate ourselves all the time. For example, when talk of auto-enrollment first hit many Human Resources departments, the response from the retirement services and corporate communities was, "You can't do that—people will storm the HR office, upset that we took money out of their paychecks." Yet we experienced just the opposite, with many people saying that they knew they should have gotten into a retirement plan but the enrollment process and the paperwork involved, plus deciding where to invest, just seemed so overwhelming. They were grateful that someone else had taken that off their plate. But as Fielding Miller pointed out, "Too often employees simply want us to tell them what to do. They just aren't willing to take ownership in planning in their own retirement. I believe the best retirement programs are created by paternalistic employers that require their employees to take an increasing responsibility for planning their own retirement future. I don't like the idea of keeping employees completely in the dark (aka auto-everything), because sooner or later they will need to make decisions, and they will be prepared only if they have been involved along the way." While there are many who would prefer others to do things for them, as was graphically represented in the BBC's *The Young Ones,* we have to consider just how much we are prepared to give up when we hand over responsibility for our lives to others.

It is time for the same directness that prompted the president who told his employees that only stupid people would fail to join the company's retirement plan—and he didn't hire stupid people. It is time for the same message that the 401(k) Whisperers take pride in conveying to plan sponsors—regardless of whether it is what they want to hear. And that same approach needs to be doled out on a national basis.

Chad Larsen asked, "What do we have to lose by putting out a very direct message?"

> *I'm 48 years old. I would be perfectly fine if this Debt Commission came out today and said, you know what, Chad? You can't retire or receive your full Social Security benefits until you're age 70. That wouldn't bother me one bit because now I know they are serious about fixing the problem and it may be there for my children.*
>
> *I may be in the minority here, but I think that when something's broken and we know it has to be fixed I'd prefer someone to tell me what my options are. At the moment I'm not so sure. The messages we are sending out are so vague and there are so many variables that it's difficult for any of us to get our arms around what we're to do.*
>
> *What do I want to happen? Just don't surprise me down the road. Just tell me so I've got time to prepare for it.*

So, what might a simple, direct, and honest message look like, based on everything we have learned about how to design an effective public service campaign? In order to discover what needs to be done to attack the retirement readiness crisis, our next question was to look at the ways in which unpalatable and unwelcome messages can be made compelling and sticky.

Chapter 9

Tell Me a Story

Reasons don't change behavior. When it comes to inspiring people to embrace some strange new change in behavior, storytelling isn't just better than the other tools. It's the only thing that works.
　　—Steve Denning, *The Science of Storytelling,* Forbes.com, 2012

I t is perfectly logical when you know the secret, yet seems almost magical when you don't.

A presenter shows the audience 12 to 15 items on a screen with no apparent connection between them. "Who claims to have a poor memory?" he asks—at which almost everyone's hands go up. The presenter selects one guinea pig whom they are going to teach—in just 15 minutes—to recite that list of items, perfectly, in the right order.

The volunteer is taken away and 15 minutes later returns, in front of the audience. This person stands with their back to the screen, the list visible to everyone but them. The presenter asks if they're ready and the volunteer nods, but seems kind of nervous. Given their previously admitted poor memory, how likely is it that they will remember the list correctly?

Yet that is exactly what they do—without fumbling or hesitation. How did they manage to remember all of those things in so short a time?

The secret to that success lies in what the volunteer was shown how to do in the time they spent behind the scenes: to create a short story out of a list of otherwise discrete items. They were exposed to one of the most profound but frequently overlooked ways in which human beings connect, communicate, and compel: storytelling.

Try it for yourself. The ability to memorize the following list within minutes is something that few of us are able to do unless we have a way to connect them:

Syracuse	crown	wreath	weight	artisan
rumors	silver	truth	cousin	mathematics
bath	volume	solution	street	Eureka

Now weave those 15 words into a story, something like this:

*One day the king of **Syracuse** decided to have a **crown** made, shaped like a **wreath**. He gave a certain **weight** of gold to a local **artisan** but soon heard **rumors** that the man had mixed it with **silver** and pocketed the difference. To discover the **truth**, the king called upon his **cousin**, a **mathematics** scholar who, lowering himself into a **bath**, noticed he displaced a **volume** of water. The **solution** became clear, at which point he rushed into the **street** shouting, **Eureka**!*

You probably recognize this as the story of how the ancient Greek mathematician discovered what has been called *Archimedes' Principle*. All you need to do to remember that list of 15 words is run through that story in your mind, visualizing each key word clearly as you do so.

Facts Aren't Everything

As Chip and Dan Heath point out in *Made to Stick: Why Some Ideas Survive and Others Die,* "A story is powerful because it provides the context missing from abstract prose." Yet business often forgets that, including the retirement services industry.

We have mistakenly thought that by providing people with factual information, they will have everything they need to take action. When that does not work, we think it is because they have not had *enough* information—so we give them more. In fact, the amount of information that is now available—factual, "abstract prose"—becomes so overwhelming that it is not surprising that many people tune out and turn off their thinking about retirement readiness.

What is the solution to achieving a different outcome? How about telling better stories? After all, it is not as if there isn't sufficient evidence as to how powerful this approach has been in influencing hearts and minds. Not just that, but stories can help to transform beliefs and shape behavior in ways that were previously thought impossible.

As renowned Hollywood screenwriting coach, Robert McKee, pointed out in a *Harvard Business Review* article entitled "Storytelling That Moves People: A Conversation with Screenwriting Coach Robert McKee": "If you can harness imagination and the principles of a well-told story, then you get people rising to their feet amid thunderous applause instead of yawning and ignoring us."

There is no disputing the fact, given our current retirement readiness statistics, that the retirement services industry is largely being ignored, despite the proliferation of information that it provides to the American public. People may not be yawning when they hear the word retirement but in all likelihood many are acting like ostriches and burying their heads in the proverbial sand hoping the issue will either go away or that someone else will come in and fix things for them. As we have illustrated throughout this book, as a society we are not as actively engaged as we need to be in order to remedy the shortfall between the savings we have accumulated (if any) and what each of us needs in order to retire in a timely and dignified manner.

But if the answer to this impasse lies in better storytelling, what exactly does that mean? To better understand the nature of effective narrative as a means of achieving a different outcome on retirement readiness, we explored how others have used storytelling, past and present, to unpack the necessary elements such as messenger, message, and medium that would be needed for an effective campaign.

We begin with an historic example of how one vitally important message—that was especially unpopular and largely ignored by the primary stakeholders (the medical profession)—gained traction in nineteenth century England.

How Florence Nightingale Changed the Medical Profession

Florence Nightingale's (1820–1910) grit and determination were evident long before she became the woman completely transformed the way the medical profession thought about army medical care, while attending to British soldiers during the Crimean War. In an era when all middle-class families (Florence was the daughter of a well-to-do English landowner) wanted was to marry their daughters off to rich husbands, Florence rejected a variety of wealthy suitors by the time she was 25, declaring that she intended to become a nurse. This further horrified her parents, as it was a job that at that time was considered suitable only for working-class women.

After completing her studies in Germany, Florence returned to England to work at a women's hospital in Harley Street, London. After Russia invaded Turkey in 1853 and dramatic stories began to be reported in *The Times* of London that close to 8,000 men in the space of just a few weeks were dying, not from shrapnel wounds but from cholera and malaria, Florence volunteered her services. Despite the high level of prejudice against women offering medical assistance of any kind, she was finally permitted to lead a group of nurses to Turkey.

What Florence discovered appalled her. The injured were left in filthy conditions without adequate warmth or decent food. In the army hospitals at that time only one in six deaths was attributable to wounds. It was disease—not war—that was killing large numbers of these soldiers.

Despite her continued appeals to the authorities that military hospitals needed to be overhauled to better deal with the real causes of soldiers' deaths, Florence was ridiculed by doctors, her professionalism attacked, and her suggestions ignored by the army top brass. Nevertheless, the British public—through the press—loved reading stories about her and when she returned to England three years later, Florence Nightingale was heralded as a national heroine not least because the death rate, following her principles of care, had dropped from 40 percent to just 2 percent.

Florence leveraged this notoriety and began a campaign to reform hospital care more broadly. Her books *Notes on Hospitals* and *Notes on Nursing,* both published in 1859, helped to completely transform the medical profession. Nightingale's message was consistent throughout because it was based on a clear vision: to target medical care at the real causes of illness—such as unsanitary conditions—rather than where doctors simply imagined them to be.

LESSONS ON STORYTELLING FROM NIGHTINGALE

Florence Nightingale was not the only person revolutionizing the way army hospitals tended the sick at that time. Yet it was her story—not others'—that prompted an outcry and much needed medical reform. The Heath brothers in *Made to Stick* refer to the Mother Teresa effect, who is reputed to have said: "If I look at the masses, I will never act. If I look at the one, I will."

It was much more compelling for British newspaper readers to hear about a single, heroic individual than a faceless group of nurses. Florence Nightingale's story was further enhanced by the moniker given to her by *Times* newspaper writers: *The Lady with the Lamp*, an image immortalized by the poet Henry Wadsworth Longfellow in his poem entitled *Santa Filomena*.

When you look more closely at the Florence Nightingale story, you can see that it adheres to the six principles of "stickiness" outlined in *Made to Stick*:

1. It is **Simple** (soldiers are dying needlessly).
2. **Unexpected** (unsanitary conditions are largely responsible for soldiers' deaths, not their wounds).
3. **Concrete** (40 percent of soldiers are dying from disease).
4. **Credible** (Nightingale was an internationally trained nurse with impeccable credentials).
5. **Emotional** (brave men are dying; a lone woman is tending to them, against all odds).
6. And presents a **Story** (the Lady with the Lamp flitting among soldiers' bedsides at night, offering comfort).

Had the Crying Indian campaign been conceived as the Crying *Indians* (as in a whole tribe) PSA, it would likely not have had the impact that it did. As human beings we are much more attracted to stories involving a single, compelling character than ones involving a group. This is because, as the Heath brothers point out in *Made to Stick,* one of the most compelling plotlines that human beings respond to is that of the David and Goliath story.

In the case of Florence Nightingale, this one woman (David) went up against the might of the established medical profession (Goliath). She succeeded in changing beliefs and thus long-standing behaviors with the help of a compelling narrative that was enhanced by the ease with which people hearing the story could instantly see a mental picture of the lady with the lamp attending to needlessly suffering soldiers.

So, who might be our David or underdog in the case of a retirement readiness story?

Interestingly, it was stories about their grandmothers (and sometimes grandfathers) that many of our interviewees reflected upon in order to personalize the concept of retirement readiness.

For example, Dallas Salisbury told us:

> *My grandfather was in the life insurance business for 40 years; I guess you could say he was a bad risk for his own company because he passed away at 66.*

> *My grandmother was 63 when he died, and she lived until she was 93. Essentially, her only income for that entire time was Social Security. She had sold her house, lived in a small apartment for those 30 years. She didn't have many of the things she'd had during her more robust life years, but she had her personal belongings around her, her collectibles around her, her furniture, her family, and her pictures. She had food on the table, a warm roof over her head, and lots to read and the ability to be happy. And I think that's what all of us in a civilized society should strive to make sure everyone can have.*

So perhaps the messenger of the retirement readiness message, spearheading a public campaign, needs to be "everyone's" grandmother? Who, then, is the Goliath she needs to go up against? Maybe it's our consumer-oriented, spendaholic society!

But any messenger needs a compelling message, story that everyone can understand and empathize with. And few are more compelling than what are called *origin stories*—which is why so many savvy business organizations capitalize on them to humanize themselves, communicate character, as well as establish the values they hold dear and inform others of the way they choose to conduct themselves.

Business and the Creation Myth

For stories to truly resonate, including in today's world of business, they must not only be compelling but also have a grain of truth.

Consider, for example, the "founded in a garage" myth still held in awe by Silicon Valley start-ups, inspired by the origins of leading high-tech businesses such as Hewlett-Packard, Google, and Apple. These stories seem to especially hit home with Americans because they reinforce the message that "regardless of how humble your beginnings are, you can turn something into an immense success story if you work hard," according to Dartmouth business professor Pino Audia who has researched the "garage" phenomenon.

Crafting a compelling origin story is so powerful that some companies have used it nefariously, such as the story that one of eBay's early employees told (falsely) that the company started because the creator wanted to help his fiancée find more of the Pez dispensers she collected. That story successfully captured the interest of reporters who otherwise had ignored the company's early PR.

One of the truths that speaks most powerfully of all for business leaders, who effectively use stories to communicate with stakeholders both inside and outside their organizations, involves those beliefs we categorize as values. The more basic these values are—including love—the more universally appealing the ensuing message is able to be.

UGLYDOLL—A LOVE STORY

David Horvath and Sun-Min Kim were forced by circumstances outside of their control to live on opposite sides of the world. After meeting at the Parsons School of Design in 1996, they fell in love. Following Sun-Min's required return to South Korea (apparently due to problems with her student visa), David would write her letters featuring a hand-drawn character named Wage alongside a message that read, "Working hard to make our dreams come true so we can be together again soon." The dream David and Sun-Min shared was to "tell stories through books and toys."

On a whim, Sun-Min took David's design and hand-sewed a plush Wage doll, which she mailed back to him in the United States. David showed it to his editor friend Eric Nakamura of *Giant Robot* magazine who at that time owned several retail stores selling dolls and other goods crafted by young creatives. Apparently Eric thought David was pitching him a product and asked him to supply a quantity of dolls to sell in the store. That was in 2001. Sun-Min quickly got to work, hand-producing two dozen of these plush dolls, including another invented character named Babo, which David delivered to *Giant Robot.*

Much to their surprise the supply sold out within a day. The rest, as they say, is history. In 2006, their company, Uglydoll received the Specialty Toy of the Year award from the Toy Industry of America and has gone on to become a highly successful international company whose dolls have inspired other merchandizing and an upcoming animated feature film. It has only benefited the company, in terms of sales and media coverage, that the Uglydoll was a product of the love between the two founders.

Communicating Values

This kind of origin story—how a global business was born from love and its founders' habit of sending each other affectionate messages—is highly coveted in the world of business, for good reason. It was easier and more compelling in Hewlett-Packard— given our propensity to attend and respond to storytelling—to spread the tale of how former CEO Bill Hewlett used a bolt cutter on the door to the supply room with instructions that it should never be locked again, in order to communicate the importance of trust within the organization. That story was always going to be much more compelling than passing down some incomprehensible edict from Human Resources.

Similarly, CEO of Cisco Systems John Chambers' admission of having grown up with a learning disability, including all of the attendant challenges that presented, like being mocked by other children and even teachers, gives an insight into the *man,* not simply the manager. It also helps to illuminate the values that he espouses around diversity and appreciation for everyone's talents that he brings to the organization.

Why are these kinds of values-infused stories so compelling? Because, as with the Florence Nightingale example, they provide us with instantly recognizable, truthful characters whom we can all relate to and identify with. And it's the nature of a hero character at the start of their venture that helps to shape the emerging organization and keep it on track.

As with all the campaigns discussed in Chapter 6, there was something about the sadness embodied in Iron Eyes Cody that the American public recognized in themselves; something deeply rooted and connective. The same held true for Rosie the Riveter, who struck a chord with women who felt that they had more to offer the world. And Christy Turlington's own story about the devastating loss of her father to lung cancer is more likely to speak to those predisposed to quit smoking than a plethora of statistics.

Yet, as Mike Figliuolo mimics in his book *One Piece of Paper: The Simple Approach to Powerful, Personal Leadership,* business and government often fail to communicate in a way that not only captures our attention but ignites our hearts.

Do you recognize this, for example, which is Figliuolo's parody of a typical organizational mission statement?

> *(Our mission) is to optimally leverage the passion of our people such that at the end of the day we maximize employee engagement to get them to think outside the box and synergistically drive value-added activities in a profit-maximizing way that is a win-win for our people, our shareholders, and our customers.*

If we are serious about changing outcomes—of impacting our deepest beliefs around retirement readiness and the dignity we want to enjoy in our later years—then we need to move away from statistics and learn to tell better stories with compelling characters that touch us.

Having briefly outlined the messenger and the message, considering plotline and relatable characters, our next question was: How do we go about setting the scene in such a way that the typical American worker realizes, "This story involves me!"

A Lesson for Retirement Readiness

How curious are those of us who are involved in designing retirement plans and making most of the decisions on what is right for the average American? Do we really know the issues well enough to come up with the right solution? For example, how commonly known is it that 65-year-old respondents to a Pew Research Center Social & Demographic

Trends survey on aging reported in 2009 they consider age 74 to be the beginning of old age. Or that the same study found that the word retirement "means different things to different people"—including, for some, working either part-time or full-time.

Indeed, we might ask: To what extent is the average American worker part of today's retirement readiness conversation? How can we expect to engage people in a story they haven't been asked to be part of?

In a recent Gaping Void blog post, cartoonist Hugh McLeod wrote: "When someone is using your product, don't ask what stories are they telling about you; ask what stories they're telling about themselves, and how your product fits into it. You'll get a far more interesting answer."

A Straw Man Campaign

The story of retirement readiness is not our story but OUR story—the one that all Americans tell together. And to better understand the stories that average American workers are telling about themselves, we need to do a better job not just of observing but directly asking *all stakeholders* how they feel about this issue. Not just with respect to what their key challenges are, but what *ideas* they have for overcoming those challenges.

To that end, we propose a straw man campaign informed by stories collected from average Americans who have a perspective on this issue. After all, social media and other technologies are making it easier for the average person to make their voice heard. And people today desperately *want* their voices to be heard, not transmitted by some faceless expert on their behalf.

The scene setting that needs to be done for a new retirement readiness story must provide a context co-created with the very people who live with this issue every day. We can deftly come up with a compelling David character and embed him in a David and Goliath tussle; we can give that character a back story (as with the garage and Uglydoll examples) that each of us would recognize because it speaks to values we all share. But if we average Americans don't latch on to the fact that this is *our* story in which *we* have a key role to play, the production—so to speak—is likely to shut down prematurely.

That is why we end this book with a letter with your name on it—one (or more) of the four that you will find in Chapter 11. But before we come to that, let's review the challenge facing us by addressing what *we* feel needs to be done. When it comes to taking action we're not simply into posing problems and suggesting some broad-brush solutions. We have already picked up the gauntlet and started running with it.

Chapter 10

Join the Dance

Unless someone like you cares a whole awful lot, nothing's going to get better. It's not.

—The Once-ler in *The Lorax* by Dr. Seuss

A few months ago after my young sons and I had just completed our monthly pilgrimage to the barber, the boys and I emerged from the Starbucks just opposite Supercuts. At 10, my youngest has developed a taste for a tall decaf mocha, which, like Amy Haley mentioned in earlier chapters, I indulge on an occasional basis. What happened next was totally unexpected and quite powerful. I caught sight of an early model Volvo parked just opposite our car. What drew my attention wasn't the fact that this was one of the older, square-shaped models or the faded paint, but the amount of stuff you wouldn't normally expect packed into a car. It looked as if an entire neighborhood was about to go on a camping trip, and this was their sole means of transportation.

I watched as an elderly woman exited the car and walked to the back holding a blanket, which she then meticulously folded before placing it inside the trunk and gently closing the lid. With a pit in my stomach I glanced over at my boys to see if they had noticed, wondering how our conversation might evolve if they had. My oldest son had a perplexed look on his face.

As we drove off, the car was quiet for the next few blocks. Then the question I had been dreading came. "Dad, does that lady live in her car?" AJ wanted to know. While the question was fully anticipated, I didn't have an answer or even know in which direction to take the discussion, so I asked, "Why do you think she lived in her car?" "Because there was a lot of stuff in there and I saw a cat," he replied. We talked the rest of the way home, but nobody was satisfied with the outcome; how could we be?

While homelessness is an issue most of us come face to face with occasionally, if not regularly, this felt very different, much closer to home. The woman's mannerisms and the way she folded that blanket were so similar to that of my own mom, who is comfortably retired. I found myself wondering, how did it happen that someone who had once bought a Volvo was now reduced to living out of it?

If this book serves to alert us to our individual and collective responsibilities concerning a more financially secure, dignified retirement for people like this, then we will have accomplished what we set out to do.

Some Honest Reflection

We can start by taking stock of our current reality. While the advent of the 401(k) and 403(b) have dramatically broadened retirement savings and are capable vehicles for carrying us forward, we have not formed the habits necessary for the average American to retire in relative comfort. In July 2012 the U.S. Senate Committee on Health, Education, Labor and Pensions reported that the retirement income deficit—that is, the difference between what people have saved for retirement and what they should have saved—is $6.6 trillion.

While crisis is a strong word that is typically reserved for things like floods, hurricanes, and famines, make no mistake that the state of our retirement readiness is in crisis! Six point six trillion dollars is a really hard number to grasp, so consider it this way: a million seconds is 12 days, a billion seconds is 31 years, and a trillion seconds is 31,688 years. Multiply that by 6.6 and you see we have some serious catching up to do.

Whereas we can (and do) quibble about whether these projections accurately reflect reality, nobody contests that our retirement readiness is hugely underfunded. We all need to take responsibility for where we are today, not just industry, policymakers, employers, and the American worker. When we know that financial literacy is not generally taught in schools, how can we expect people to understand the importance of saving for their future? And *that* is the responsibility of us all. When consumerism is not just valued in our society but revered—and saving isn't—is our current predicament so very surprising?

Let's imagine a future when financial education is embedded in schools on a national basis. When courses similar to Mathew Frost's personal finance game are being taught in every school in the country, instilling students with the confidence to know that basic financial acumen is not just something that we can all acquire, but can be fun and satisfying too.

By learning skills like budgeting, saving, and investing, students can change their beliefs about their ability to plan for the future. Changing beliefs helps to change behavior so that in the future we help to create a nation of savers, especially more of those confident Super Savers we mentioned in Chapter 1.

The concepts surrounding retirement planning are more complex than that, however, and no amount of financial education is going to mitigate the problem entirely. While understanding that key principles of sound saving and investing are fundamental, we also have to do a better job of simplifying what each person needs to know to achieve a uniquely relevant and successful outcome. That means simplifying worksite savings plans as well. As all of our interviewees agreed, a comfortable retirement should not be dependent upon investment acumen but should be available to anyone who works hard and saves diligently for it.

A Vision for Workplace Savings

What, then, is our vision? It needs to start by acknowledging that voluntary worksite savings programs, like the 401(k) and 403(b), have become Americans' predominant retirement savings vehicles. As such, success is currently defined in adoption rates, both by employers and employees; this success metric needs to embrace higher savings rates as well.

It is with this in mind that I propose the simple vision of a 10 percent lifetime savings rate across America.

Now, I suspect that a 10 percent lifetime savings rate seems incredibly audacious to some and far too little to others, but it is simple and ambitious by today's savings standards and would have a profound impact on this nation's retirement readiness in a relatively short space of time.

Rather than fragment the industry by coming up with our own individual prescription for success, thereby negating the considerable thought and viable solutions on the table currently, we suggest an approach inspired by improvisational theatre. It's known as the *yes and . . .* technique. It is the principle that first you accept a gift (the *yes*) then you build on it (the *and*). In fact, the 10 percent savings rate mentioned above is by no means novel, it is in fact a "yes and . . ." to others who have made this statement many times before. Here's what we mean by "yes and . . ." as far as the individual concepts of coverage, plan performance metrics, leakage, and longevity previously outlined in Chapter 7 are concerned.

COVERAGE

As Mark Iwry from the U.S. Treasury stressed during our discussions, if people are left to their own devices outside of a workplace savings plan, a change in retirement readiness is not going to happen. We need to make sure that all workers have the ability to save through payroll deduction in the workplace. Today, the percentage of workers who are *unable* to participate in an employer-sponsored retirement plan is 40 percent (2010 DOL Population Survey). We need to chip away at that figure—and do it today—by engaging all constituencies in this debate.

Let's begin by agreeing (saying yes) that our vision is 100 percent workplace coverage. And? That's for all the stakeholders to decide.

PLAN PERFORMANCE METRICS

In his book *Save More Tomorrow*, mentioned in Chapter 7, UCLA professor of Behavioral Finance Shlomo Benartzi prescribed a simple set of metrics for an effective retirement plan; 90–10–90, which implies:

- ◆ 90 percent employee participation in the company's retirement plan.
- ◆ 10 percent average contribution rate by employees.

◆ 90 percent of employees selecting (or default investing into) a simple, one-stop, professionally managed portfolio (such as a target date solution).

What if we universally adopted these metrics as a benchmark for plan success? Could we get to our 10 percent savings rates? Again, to this we say "Yes and. . . ."

Leakage

Legislation was introduced in the 112th Congress to help reduce leakage from the defined contribution retirement system, known as the SEAL Act (Savings Enhancement by Alleviating Leakage in 401(k) Savings Act of 2011). Again, protecting already established retirement plan balances from leaking out of the retirement system is an important step toward retirement readiness. To this we say, "Yes and. . . ."

Longevity

To help protect retirees from the prospect of outliving their assets, new retirees should be exposed to the concept of longevity risk pooling, whether through investing in a lifetime income benefit such as an annuity, through longevity insurance, or some other form of guaranteed product. We fully agree that longevity is an issue that needs to be addressed and we support these protections with an emphatic "Yes, and. . . ."

Fostering New Behaviors

Having outlined the behavior we are looking to motivate while acknowledging the gap between this and our current reality, it is clear that a very different behavior is needed to move us closer to our desired outcome. The good news is, that while changing beliefs may prove to be a fresh (but necessary) challenge, the context surrounding a worksite retirement plan is relatively easy to control and can pay big dividends.

Ellen Langer's research, encapsulated in the BBC television program, *The Young Ones*, mentioned in Chapter 7, showed that changing the context of an individual's experience can dramatically change their beliefs and hence their behavior.

Similarly, by fostering a retirement plan environment where it is easier for an individual to save for retirement than not, we envision dramatically changing that individual's behavior around saving and investing. The retirement plan industry has already begun to adopt auto-plan features that we know profoundly change participant behavior. These auto-solutions transform a powerful force called inertia from a negative to a positive resource by turning the default from nonparticipation to participation, in addition to defaulting other valuable behaviors in the right direction.

But in addition to showing us the power of context, *The Young Ones* also cautioned us about its temporary nature. Remember that when helpers were provided to the celebrities, they started to revert back to their old ways. When context changed, so did behavior. With the median tenure of an employee being just shy of five years, an employee's context will change repeatedly throughout their working lifetime. This means that any lasting behavioral change needs to be grounded not only in context, but in beliefs; and changing beliefs isn't easy.

Some would say you simply cannot change people's beliefs about saving in a meaningful enough way to have a material impact on retirement readiness. But really, how hard have we tried to change our beliefs? Have you seen that award-winning PSA about saving for retirement? Neither have we. Why not? Because it doesn't yet exist. We managed to decrease forest fires to secure the environment; to decrease smoking to reduce lung cancer and other cigarette-induced diseases; to decrease litter to ameliorate pollution; and we got people to buckle up, reducing vehicular deaths. These were all things critics said beforehand were virtually impossible to do. Yet we achieved them. How? With simple yet compelling messages like Rosie the Riveter and Smokey Bear. We told stories, didn't we? And more than that, we got them to stick, similar to the means of remembering Florence Nightingale as the Lady with the Lamp or Hewlett Packard as "Made in a Garage."

Yes, we have to change the context within the voluntary retirement plan. And, we have to tell Americans a story that is carefully designed to stick.

Upping Our Resolve

As we mentioned in the State of the Union chapter, when John F. Kennedy finished laying out his four-part plan for space exploration, he said something very important, which is why we're repeating it here:

> *Let it be clear that I am asking the Congress and the country to accept a firm commitment to a new course of action, a course which will last for many years and carry very heavy costs: $531 million in fiscal '62—an estimated $7 to $9 billion additional over the next five years. If we are to go only half way, or reduce our sights in the face of difficulty, in my judgment it would be better not to go at all.*

President Kennedy had the foresight to immunize Congress and our nation against the potential for the lowered resolve that he knew might prevent his vision taking shape. Had he not done so, NASA, which was devoted to space exploration and the Command Center that brought Apollo 13 back to Earth, may very well have fractured and failed in its mission to send a manned spacecraft to the Moon and bring it safely back.

Similarly, if we are to succeed with retirement readiness, we will need to be crystal clear in our direction (our vision) and steadfast in our resolve during the many tests and setbacks yet to come. We need to immunize ourselves against the doubters and the skeptics who are out there. How? By bringing them to the table and saying, "Help us determine a solution—or shut the heck up!" In this case, resolve is about more than just weathering doubt and silencing skeptics; it's about leveraging that doubt and skepticism so we can craft an even better and persistent vision—and innovate around that.

We know that by changing the context of a retirement plan, we can foster a better savings environment for workers through supporting powerful retirement plan drivers that promote higher levels of saving. But we also know that not enough of these behavioral drivers are being included in retirement plans and that even when they are, they are being too timidly employed, as is the case with auto-enrollment at a default contribution rate of 3 percent. We also know that in order to fully utilize these drivers, we will need to see a shift in focus for the entire industry: plan sponsors, financial advisors, and policy makers.

These kinds of changes will demand a strong resolve from all stakeholders, because they often require more effort and can even drive up plan costs.

Speaking of tough conversations, the financial services industry needs to be willing to have these with their clients, engaging employers about their plan's effectiveness in truly promoting retirement readiness. Employers, in turn, must believe that it is their responsibility to encourage workers to save for retirement and be willing to make bold changes to their retirement plans. And policymakers must support these drivers for retirement plan success by making them easier to adopt.

Again, we don't mean to insinuate that everything that has already been suggested or implemented needs to be scrapped. On the contrary, in the spirit of "Yes, and . . ." we're asking for a broader, more cohesive national conversation.

As University of California, Davis professor Andrew Hargadon outlines in his book *How Breakthroughs Happen: The Surprising Truth About How Companies Innovate*: "The notion of the lone genius laboring away in the basement laboratory to invent a future is, by now, one we should all be safely free of. Innovative firms succeed not by breaking free from the constraints of the past, but instead by harnessing the past in powerful new ways. The result is an innovation process that thrives by making smaller bets, by building the future from what's already at hand."

In short, while we need to look for creative input both within our industry as well as outside of it, we need to recognize the progress we've made and resist the temptation some feel to throw the baby out with the bath water. Further, we need to recognize that our answers will likely come from a concept Hargadon refers to as "Recombinant Innovation," which simply stated involves the recombining of old ideas, rather than inventing completely new ones.

So what are we going to do about it?

There is nothing worse than the person who speculates and complains about all that is wrong, postulates a few solutions, and then sits on their hands doing nothing. It's time to seriously get to work. We know that context drives behavior and behavior can drive beliefs, but what catalyst do we need to begin transforming our culture from a nation of spenders to a nation of Super Savers?

How do we transform beliefs so that our industry begins to reestablish the context of worksite plans in a way that truly promotes saving?

How do we convince employers to take on that new level of paternalism/maternalism required to embrace the bold new plan design?

And how do we create the motivation needed for the American worker to simply save more?

While we know inertia plays a significant role, unless our society possesses a strong belief that saving for retirement is important, distractions will derail the best of intentions over the long term.

A broader movement is needed to capture the hearts and minds of Americans, and a new idealism needs to take root to create the same habits around saving as have been created around brushing our teeth. The ingenuity that has been demonstrated around the 60-year history of public service movements in America, that addressed such important topics as littering, smoking, and the wearing of seat belts, needs to be applied to one of the most important crises of the twenty-first century: retirement readiness.

What, then, do we suggest as a jumping off point?

Our proposal is for the financial services industry to form a coalition with policymakers, similar to what happened to drive the Keep America Beautiful campaign, with the single mission of ensuring every American has the opportunity to save and retire with dignity. This coalition will need to be 100 percent brand agnostic with respect to the products and services of its underlying members and coalesce around the need to save above all else.

Simple concepts, such as saving 10 percent of your pay annually, which are easy to remember and simple to explain, need to be scripted and repeated with the kind of frequency that produces stickiness. By leveraging traditional, social, and digital media in new and refreshing ways, we can begin to plant the seed needed to change our national beliefs around saving for retirement and retirement readiness. Social media engines such as Facebook, Twitter, LinkedIn, YouTube, Pinterest, and the like can be harnessed to propagate these themes, similar to the way that they have helped to impact recent world events.

To continue the conversation started within this book, we have established a website at www.SavingAmerica.org. Designed to put beliefs into action, this brand agnostic site is intended to serve as a hub for helping to gather ideas and spread the word about effective workplace retirement savings programs in America.

Visit www.SavingAmerica.org today to learn how you can become a champion of the national movement to build a more secure retirement.

The Dancing Man

I recently attended a leadership program at Duke University where one concept stood out: the fact that our society celebrates The Dancing Man. This is the innovator, the person who steps outside the box to be the catalyst for change. Our society recognizes this person as very important—perhaps the most important; in fact, we often assign to them an almost heroic persona. But one individual does not make a movement, and so this is somewhat of a naïve interpretation. More often than not, it is the first person to join the dance—the first follower—who begins to tip a movement, because one person dancing alone is just a lone nut!

Look on YouTube for Derek Sivers' remarkable short video, *First Follower: Leadership Lessons from the Dancing Guy* and watch what happens as the lone dancing nut becomes the inspiration for an entire movement. You'll notice how the momentum really picks up steam as the third and fourth dancers join in and everything tips.

We know we are in the throes of a retirement readiness crisis and the challenge is of epic proportions. On January 1, 2011, the oldest people within the Baby Boomer generation began turning 65 years of age. Ten thousand more will join them, every day, for the next 19 years, as reported by the Pew Research Center. An estimated third of Americans aged 62 or older say that they have "already delayed retirement because of the recession."

Yet despite the graying of the labor force, we need to reassure ourselves that the story has not yet played out—it's not over quite yet because the complete story has not yet been written. It is ultimately the responsibility of each one of us to help get the ending right. But, in order for us to make true and lasting change, we are going to have to create a society-wide movement.

So what are we asking you to do? Simply this: join the dance. And if you are still not sure how, just turn the page because in the final chapter of this book there is a letter from me with your name on it.

Chapter **11**

Letters to Stakeholders

This chapter offers a letter to each of the four main groups we believe need to help enact the change to a more retirement ready America. Please read them all and then go back to the letter that speaks directly to you. Beyond that, make a conscious decision to have a voice in this vital, national conversation.

As Andy Warhol pointed out in *Andy Warhol in His Own Words:* "When people are ready to, they change. They never do it before then, and sometimes they die before they get around to it. You can't make them change if they don't want to, just like when they do want to, you can't stop them."

Which of those people are you?

Letter to all Americans

Dear fellow Americans,

When the National Foundation for Credit Counseling (NFCC) recently polled Americans just like you about their greatest financial regrets, guess what were the top three responses?

1. Habitually overspending.
2. Inadequately saving.
3. Not saving enough for retirement.

Chances are that you relate to one or all of these issues, so let's try a brief thought experiment.

Imagine you could go back in time 20, 30, maybe even 40 years, to the point at which you have just begun to work. Given what you feel now about the inadequacy of your retirement savings—or even your financial security in general—what would you do differently? Would you be inclined to question your need for all that stuff you habitually bought over the years? To set aside whatever you could—but at least 10 percent—of your earnings? To take advantage of whatever retirement plan your employer offered, and then roll it over to the next plan when you moved on to a different job?

Of course, with hindsight, very few of us would refuse to do some or all of those things. Unfortunately, we don't have the luxury of going back to change what we did in the past. What we *do* have, however, is the ability to change the future. Here's how.

Forget your own situation for a moment. Can you imagine how much more inclined you would have been to save for the future if someone you knew and admired had taken you aside and told you how they now regretted not starting to save sooner?

What if your future self had explained the consequences of living each day, knowing that there is very little time and energy left to secure that dream you always had? Including retiring when you choose to, rather than having to continue working because otherwise you just don't have enough to live on?

Why not be that future self to a young person in your life—starting today? And, yes, we're aware that young folks are not always the most receptive to wise advice, so maybe you should start even sooner than you would think.

You might begin by downloading *Money As You Grow: 20 Things Kids Need To Know To Live Financially Smart Lives,* the document we mention in Chapter 5 on financial literacy, available at www.money asyougrow.org/and take inspiration from the milestones outlined in that booklet.

Why aren't you the person who helps teach our very youngest citizens that they may have to wait before buying what they want? Or who shares the wonders of compound interest with a pre-teen? Or who uses the challenges of funding college as a way to bring a teenager into important financial discussions? Or who makes their graduation gift to a new entrant into our workforce a sum of money with which to open a savings account or some form of IRA?

Remember Amy Haley from Chapter 1 and how she was strongly influenced by her grandfather with respect to the way he invested and managed his money—to the extent that he had left his widow comfortably off? Wouldn't you want any young person you care about to have the kind of freedom and options of someone like that, who habitually puts away between 10 and 20 percent of her income and doesn't feel like she's missing out? On the contrary, think about what your life would be like now, with all the dreams you could bring into reality, if you had started saving right from the get-go.

You know one of the coolest things about paying it forward in this way? We all know that actions speak louder than words, right? Then it won't be enough for you to embrace the typical "do as I say, not as I do" mantel of parenting. By researching the issue of financial literacy in order to offer a young person wise counsel, you could end up finding that you have changed your own beliefs and behaviors and can look forward to a more secure retirement than would otherwise have been the case.

There are many things we don't—or won't—do for ourselves. But when it comes to our children, or those young people we care about the most, we would walk over coals to make their lives the best they can be, wouldn't we? Then consider this: think about what you most regret and be darned sure that you won't allow those in your care and loving influence to experience the same when they reach your age. Start them saving—today!

Letter to Plan Sponsors

Dear Plan Sponsor/Employer,

I have had the pleasure of working directly for (and with) you for the past 35 years. I know you to be inherently good people who care about the success of your businesses, the products and services you deliver, and yes, you care about the employees who serve your organizations. You likely spend as much time with your employees as you do your own families. You become vested in their lives and their success, both present and future. One of the very best ways you can help positively to influence their future success is to get them to save for retirement.

Imagine for a moment you are 20 years in the future and that you are retired. You took retirement planning seriously from a very early age and have reached financial critical mass, the point at which your savings will clearly outlast you and your family. Congratulations! You have clearly made some good decisions and represent a small minority of our society. Life is good for you.

Let's further imagine that it's a special occasion and you've invited a few close friends to join you for dinner at your favorite restaurant, which is in a rough part of town. You have just parked the car—your spouse and friends having already made their way into the restaurant so as not to get wet—when you spin around and accidentally bump into a homeless man who is hunched over and soaked to the bone. Although there is something strangely familiar about him, you rush for the warmth of the restaurant.

As the maître d' seats you, your memory comes rushing back. You realize the man was Bill, who worked for you for 10 years. He was kind, loyal, and a very hard worker. You sit there in silence wondering how something like this could possibly happen. The sad truth is that there may be Bills in every one of our companies.

Okay, so I'm channeling my inner Dickens here to labor the point. But let me ask you this: how many of our current employees could end up like Bill? Unfortunately, if the current statistics are anything to go by, this may not be as unusual as one might hope. Remember the woman who was told by Paul D'Aiutolo that she had to continue working because she had no savings to retire on? She is just one of millions of Americans—tens of millions—who have next to nothing set aside, not just for their retirement but for anything at all. In fact, a recent study indicated that half of Americans have three months' salary or less socked away for an emergency, and a quarter have no rainy day money to rely on at all. And the news isn't much better with the younger generation (18–29-year-olds), 63 percent of whom said they had three months' salary to cover them at best, should they lose their jobs.

So, what's this got to do with you?

Well, as we've stressed throughout this book, the workplace is the one arena in which we know we can encourage the average American to save. So, as an employer you represent America's best hope for helping your fellow citizens enjoy a dignified, secure retirement. But that means you need to adopt a retirement plan, preferably with auto-enrollment, and have a strategy in place—worked out with a skilled advisor—to help maximize every employee's retirement readiness.

We've talked a lot already about the importance of establishing the right context as a driver of behavioral change. With the Keep America Beautiful campaign, for example, the presence and proximity of garbage cans was one of the biggest influencers that changed littering behavior. This great country of ours is relying on you, then, to put in place the equivalent context for your retirement plan in order to boost retirement savings behavior in your company.

Now, let's address the elephant in the room directly. I imagine many of you are reading this and thinking that we live in a land of free choice. Some people make bad choices and we can't force them to save. You're not a parent to your employees; you are their employer. The trouble is, millions of American workers never got the memo and they are confused by the shift from defined benefit plans to defined contribution plans. Most have never been educated to understand basic financial issues—as we articulated in Chapter 5—and have never been taught to make sound financial decisions.

We've already offered you a book full of good reasons to help the people you employ maximize their retirement readiness. We've laid out the importance of increasing participation in this country to 90 percent; stressed the need for double-digit deferral rates; and outlined the value of 90 percent of employees investing their assets in simple, target date solutions that promote proper asset allocation.

But let's bring the argument back to the basic, fundamental human issue we're really talking about here. When it comes to having a retirement savings plan that will change the destiny for millions of Bills and Marys in our country we only have this to say: it's the right thing to do!

So, what will you do, and do today, to help America change its savings habit?

Letter to Policymakers

Dear Policymaker,

Those of us who have had the honor and privilege of visiting Washington, DC to converse with those parties directly involved with retirement issues cannot fail to be humbled by the passion many of you exude. There is no doubt in my mind that those who seek and attain high political office believe with every fiber of their being that they are doing what is right for this great country of ours. And when it comes to the issue of retirement we need only look to the bipartisan efforts on this important issue, led by Senators Portman and Cardin, for inspiration.

As the editors of *PLANSPONSOR* magazine, bemoaning the lack of earlier political interest in pension legislation, let alone the skills or clout necessary to effect policy, wrote in April 2003:

> *Two very different congressmen changed all that, and their hand is to be seen in virtually every piece of pension legislation this past decade. Rob Portman, a Republican from Ohio, and Ben Cardin, a Maryland Democrat, neither of notably centrist leanings, nonetheless found common cause in tackling the increasingly precarious state of workplace retirement. Working hand in hand, they managed to forge something of a consensus in a Congress that resists encroachment from the right (savings should be an individual, not a workplace, priority) and left (savings should be mandated)—and in the middle of one of the more fractious periods in American politics. Instead of the usual compromised mish-mash, their cooperation has produced what virtually all concerned recognize as intelligent and proactive pensions reform.*

Nevertheless, in concluding that article, the *PLANSPONSOR* editors added that while foreign policy should be above politics, "(p)ension policy will never have that luxury . . ."

But it can and it must—with your help!

Please—be pro-retirement savings, which on the face of it sounds like an unnecessary, even odd thing to say. But the fact is, there is a misconception in this country that we are not just a spending culture, but our government *needs* us to be a spending culture, otherwise the economy will collapse. And, sadly, that misconception persists despite the fact that we know that our citizens need to be saving more—not just for the sake of themselves and their families—but in order to establish and maintain a buoyant economy over the long haul.

Which segues into the real message of this letter. Yes, I could stress how we need your help with issues like coverage. We really could do with simplifying many of the rules around auto-enrollment. And greater legislative focus on financial literacy is, as we illustrated in Chapter 5, not only hugely important but perhaps needs to take a more upbeat and aggressive stance than previously. But you've read the book and presumably know that all of these things are within your purview.

The real point is how vital it is to take the *long view* with the issue of retirement readiness. We need a compelling vision that takes into account context *and* beliefs, in order to ensure that working Americans can retire with dignity, with sufficient savings, and the option to give up work when they choose. Not a four-year or even an eight-year vision . . . but one that spans many generations to come!

How? Well, Washington already has the context and beliefs in place to do exactly that. I stumbled upon the U.S. Office of Personnel Management's website that has been set up for "recruiting, retaining, and honoring a world-class workforce to serve the American people." Some of the competencies listed "to build a federal corporate culture that drives for results, serves customers, and builds successful teams and coalitions . . ." are:

- ◆ Creativity and innovation.
- ◆ Flexibility.
- ◆ Vision.
- ◆ Leveraging diversity (including, presumably, diverse opinions on how problems can be solved).
- ◆ Customer service.
- ◆ Entrepreneurship (including taking "calculated risks at accomplishing organizational objectives").
- ◆ Partnering to build coalitions.

Those are fine goals around a compelling vision. Let's apply them to the issue of retirement readiness—today! In which case, there are only two questions I have left to ask you:

1. What can you do around the issue of retirement readiness for your fellow Americans that embraces the competencies listed above?
2. What gestures and actions will you make that involve less of the fist raising we've seen in politics lately, and more about extending our hands across the current partisan divide?

Washington expects exemplary behavior from its workforce and we expect no less from our elected officials.

Letter to the Retirement Industry

Dear fellow Retirement Services Industry Professional,

Some years ago I worked as a financial advisor for Dean Witter Reynolds in the San Francisco Bay Area, where I built my client base by offering educational seminars on financial planning in the workplace. My offer, post-presentation, was a no fee, no obligation financial assessment for anyone who wanted me to dig deeper into their financial situation; some went on to become clients.

One morning, after just such an event at a high-tech company, I met with two sets of employees. The first was an older gentleman who told me that he was looking forward to retiring soon because he had a number of lifelong dreams still to accomplish. Tentatively, he laid his financial statements on the table between us. While he wasn't rich by any means, it was immediately apparent that he was a saver. His house was paid off, he had no debt, and there was a tidy sum of money set aside. It was quite clear that his intention to retire could be met, pretty much whenever he chose; we parted company with both of us feeling good about that outcome.

Not surprisingly, I was optimistic when my second appointment of the day knocked on the door. In came a couple, around the same age, who also wanted to retire, but for quite different reasons. Neither of them was in the best of health and they told me they were just plain worn down by a lifetime of work. Their plan was to move to a place in Nevada to enjoy the drier climate and lower cost of living. Looking at their paperwork I could see that this wasn't going to happen any time soon. They had $50,000 in savings between them but considerable credit card debt and a timeshare that was proving difficult to offload. A quick calculation put their net worth close to zero. But here's the really stunning fact—they were dumbfounded when I delivered the message, completely unaware of their predicament.

Tell me, how does that happen? In the face of rampant consumerism and free-flowing revolving debt, as Paul D' Aiutolo so eloquently stated, "We just have to do better. We have to do better as an industry to not have people be in that position."

Never mind the industry as a whole—what about you? What are you doing to ensure that the people you serve never find themselves in that position? You want to know how the people who Charlie Ruffel calls 401(k) Whisperers do it? In short, they don't back down.

What do I mean by that? Well, here's the thing. How many times have you asked a plan sponsor if they've considered auto-enrollment—one thing that we know drives participation in workplace retirement plans? And how many times have you heard from them that it's too expensive and so they're not going to do that right now?

That's the moment of truth. What do you do then? Do you say, "Okay, I understand that, let's look at other options," or do you stand your ground? Do you point out to them that we all have to do something about this retirement readiness crisis in the United States by ensuring maximum participation in workplace plans —otherwise people will have nothing saved for when they retire? Do you challenge their responsibility to their employees, or just look the other way and carry on as if it's not your—or their—ultimate responsibility?

If being in this business for over 20 years has taught me anything, it's that we each have the ability to profoundly shape the behavior of plan sponsors. Just look at where we have done that already: plan investment fund selection and fiduciary risk mitigation being just two examples. We not only built the solutions—the tool sets, processes, and standards—we created the demand for them by doggedly emphasizing fiduciary liability and the need for investment due diligence.

Now, I'm not suggesting that these things aren't important; of course they are. But, having read this book wouldn't you agree that, in the great scheme of things, they are certainly not the most important things we could be stressing to plan sponsors? How the one thing that will help change outcomes would be to get more people into a workplace retirement savings plan in the first place? It's time that we as an industry focus our innovative energy around the things that matter most: get everyone to participate, drive up deferral rates, and direct them to fundamentally sound investment choices. These are the things that will move the needle.

So, I ask you again: What are you prepared to do about that? When the moment of truth comes and a plan sponsor kicks back against designing a plan for maximum participation with the "too expensive" argument—what do you do then? Challenge or conform?

As the former Chairman and CEO of IBM Thomas J. Watson once said, "If you stand up and be counted, from time to time you may get yourself knocked down. But remember this: A man flattened by an opponent can get up again. A man flattened by conformity stays down for good."

For the sake not just of your own ability to sleep at night, but for the good of our industry long term *and* the sake of this country and its citizens, we cannot stay down for much longer on this issue.

A 401(k) Whisperer. That's a pretty cool term for those men and women who *are making a real difference in people's lives.*

So—here are two questions directed specifically to you: Will you join us? Then how will you prove you deserve to?

Bibliography

401k Help Center. "The SEAL Act: A Senate Bill Designed to Reduce 401(k) Leakage," www.401khelpcenter.com/press_2011/pr_seal-act_051811.html.

TheTruth.com. *About Truth*, www.thetruth.com.

Ad Council. *Pollution: Keep America Beautiful—Iron Eyes Cody*, www.adcouncil .org/Our-Work/The-Classics/Pollution-Keep-America-Beautiful-Iron-Eyes-Cody.

Ad Council. *Seat Belt Education*, www.adcouncil.org/Our-Work/The-Classics/ Safety-Belt-Education.

Ad Council. *Wildfire Prevention*, www.adcouncil.org/Our-Work/Current-Work/ Family-Community/Wildfire-Prevention.

Ad Council. *Women in War Jobs*, www.adcouncil.org/Our-Work/The-Classics/ Women-in-War-Jobs.

Aleiss, Angela. "Native Son: After a Career as Hollywood's Noble Indian Hero, Iron Eyes Cody Is Found to Have an Unexpected Heritage." *The New Orleans Times-Picayune*, 1996.

Aluminum Association. "The Infinitely Recyclable Aluminum Can," www.aluminum.org/ Content/NavigationMenu/TheIndustry/PackagingConsumerProductMarket/Can/ default.htm.

American Institute of Certified Public Accountants. *Feed the Pig*, www.feedthepig.org.

American Recovery and Reinvestment Act of 2009. Public Law 111-5, 111th Cong., 2009.

Apollo 13. Universal Pictures movie, directed by Ron Howard. 1995.

Audia, Pino G., and Christopher I. Rider. "A Garage and an Idea: What More Does an Entrepreneur Need?" *California Management Review*. (2005), http://mba.tuck .dartmouth.edu/pages/faculty/pino.audia/docs/garage%20myth%20CMR.pdf.

Bach, David. "The Latte Factor®," www.finishrich.com/lattefactor.

Bandura, Albert. "Self-Efficacy: Toward a Unifying Theory of Behavior Change." *Psychological Review 84*, no. 2 (1977): 191–215.

Beinhocker, Eric D., Diana Farrell, and Ezra Greenberg. *Why Baby Boomers Will Need to Work Longer*. McKinsey Global Institute, www.mckinseyquarterly.com/ Why_baby_boomers_will_need_to_work_longer_2234.

Benartzi, Shlomo. *Save More Tomorrow: Practical Behavioral Finance Solutions to Improve 401(k) Plans*. New York: Penguin Group, 2012.

Beyer, Lisa. The Rise and Fall of Employer-Sponsored Retirement Plans. Workforce, http://www. workforce. com/article/20120206/WORKFORCE90/120129977/the-rise-and-fall-of-employer-sponsored-pension-plans.

Bogdan, Michael, Sarah Holden, and Daniel Schrass. "Characteristics of Mutual Fund Investors, 2011." *ICI Research Perspective 17*, no. 6, 2011.

Blakely, Stephen. *Younger 401(k) Participants Turning to Target Date Funds.* Washington, DC: Employee Benefit Research Institute, 2012.

Bureau of Census. "Labor Force Statistics from the Current Population Survey," www .bls.gov/cps.

Burson-Marsteller and Penn Schoen Berland. *2011 Crisis Preparedness Study,* www .burson-marsteller.com/CrisisResearch/.

Bush, George W. "Executive Order: Establishing the President's Council on Financial Literacy." The White House Archives, http://georgewbush-whitehouse.archives .gov/news/releases/2008/01/20080122-1.html.

Cantore, Tara. "Canadian Baby Boomers Regret Not Saving Earlier." *PLANSPONSOR*, www.plansponsor.com/Canadian_Baby_Boomers_Regret_not_Saving_Earlier .aspx.

Carstensen, Laura L. "Retirement in an Era of Long Life." *The Street*, www.thestreet .com/story/11399835/1/retirement-in-an-era-of-long-life.html.

Coffman, Julia. *Public Communication Campaign Evaluation: An Environmental Scan of Challenges, Criticisms, Practice, and Opportunities. Communications Consortium Media Center*, Harvard Family Research Project, www.hfrp .org/publications-resources/browse-our-publications/public-communication-campaign-evaluation-an-environmental-scan-of-challenges-criticisms-practice-and-opportunities.

Container Recycling Institute. "Bottle Bill Resource Guide," www.bottlebill.org.

Container Recycling Institute. "Keep America Beautiful: A History," http://toolkit .bottlebill.org/opposition/KABhistory.htm.

Copeland, Craig. "Employment Based Retirement Plan Participation: Geographic Differences and Trends, 2010." *Employee Benefit Research Institute*, no. 363, 2011.

Costa, Dora L. *The Evolution of Retirement: An American Economic History, 1880–1990.* Chicago: The University of Chicago Press, 1998.

Council of Economic Advisors. *Supporting Retirement for American Families.* Executive Office of the President, 2012.

Cushing, Harvey. *The Life of Sir William Osler, Volume 1.* Hamburg: Severus Verlag, 2010.

deMause, Neil. "Startup Lies Companies Tell You." *CNNMoney*, http://money .cnn.com/galleries/2011/smallbusiness/1103/gallery.business_creation_myths/ index.html.

Denning, Steve. "The Science of Storytelling." *Forbes*, 2012, www.forbes.com/sites/ stevedenning/2012/03/09/the-science-of-storytelling/.

Dr. Seuss. *The Lorax.* New York: Random House, 1971.

Dr. Seuss. *Oh, the Places You'll Go!* New York: Random House, 1960.

Duhigg, Charles. *The Power of Habit: Why We Do What We Do In Life and Business.* New York: Random House, 2012.

Earth Day Network. "Earth Day: The History of a Movement," www.earthday .org/earth-day-history-movement.

Economic Growth and Tax Relief Reconciliation Act of 2001. Public Law 107-16, 107th Cong., 2001.

Economic Stimulus Act of 2008. Public Law 110-185, 110th Cong., 2d sess. (2008).

Federal Reserve. "Federal Reserve Statistical Release." Consumer Credit, www.federal reserve.gov/releases/g19/Current/g19.pdf.

Fidelity Investments. *Auto-Enrollment and WSJ Article: The Rest of the Story.* Fidelity Thought Leadership, 2011.

Figliuolo, Mike. *One Piece of Paper: The Simple Approach to Powerful, Personal Leadership.* San Francisco: Jossey-Bass, 2011, 15.

Ford, Gerald. "Statement on the Employee Retirement Income Security Act of 1974." The American Presidency Project, www.presidency.ucsb.edu/ws/?pid=4679.

Freedman, Marc. *Encore: Finding Work that Matters in the Second Half of Life.* New York: Public Affairs, 2007.

Fryer, Bronwyn. *Storytelling that Moves People: A Conversation with Screenwriting Coach Robert McKee,* http://hbr.org/2003/06/storytelling-that-moves-people/ ar/1.

Gladwell, Malcolm. *Outliers: The Story of Success.* New York: Little, Brown and Company, 2008.

Governor's Highway Safety Association. "Seat Belt Laws," www.ghsa.org/html/ stateinfo/laws/seatbelt_laws.html.

Graebner, William. *A History of Retirement: The Meaning and Function of an American Institution, 1885–1978.* New Haven: Yale University Press, 1984.

Graham, Nick. "Starting to Get Crowded in 100-Year-Olds' Club." *Huffington Post,* www.huffingtonpost.com/2009/07/19/starting-to-get-crowded-i_1_n_239965.html.

Graves, Philip. *Consumerology: The Market Research Myth, the Truth About Consumers, and the Psychology of Shopping.* Boston: Nicholas Brealey Publishing, 2010, 53.

Greenspan, Alan. "Inspirational Quotes." Entheos.com, www.entheos.com/quotes/ by_topic/financial.

Hargadon, Andrew. *How Breakthroughs Happen: The Surprising Truth About How Companies Innovate.* Boston: Harvard Business School Publishing, 2003.

Harkin, Senator Tom. *The Retirement Crisis and the Plan to Resolve It.* U.S. Senate Committee on Health, Education, Labor and Pensions, 2012.

Heath, Chip, and Dan Heath. *Made to Stick: Why Some Ideas Survive and Others Die.* New York: Random House, 2007, 214.

Hill, Gladwin. "Environmental Crisis May Eclipse Vietnam as College Issue." *New York Times*, September 29, 1969.

Holden, Sarah, Jack VanDerhei, Luis Alonso, and Steven Bass. "401(k) Plan Asset Allocation, Account Balances, and Loan Activity in 2010." *ICI Research Perspective 17*, no. 10, 2011.

Hufner, Martin. "What Would Bismarck Have Done?" The Globalist.com, www.theglobalist.com/StoryId.aspx?StoryId=3615.

Illumination Entertainment News Release, http://press.uglydolls.com/2012/images/Illumination%20Entertainment%20taking%20UGLYDOLL%20to%20the%20Movies%20and%20Beyond_5.26.11.pdf.

Innocentive.com. "What We Do." www.innocentive.com/about-innocentive.

Institutional Investor. "Backing Off." InstitutionalInvestor.com, www.institutionalinvestor.com/Popups/PrintArticle.aspx?ArticleID=1027475.

Investment Company Institute. "401(k) Plans: A 25 Year Retrospective." Investment Company Institute, *Research Perspective 12*, no. 2, 2006.

Jain, Naveen. "Rethinking the Concept of 'Outliers': Why Non-Experts are Better at Disruptive Innovation." *Forbes*, www.forbes.com/sites/singularity/2012/07/12/rethinking-the-concept-of-outliers-why-non-experts-are-better-at-disruptive-innovation.

James, William. Goodreads.com, www.goodreads.com/quotes/622643-all-our-life-so-far-as-it-has-definite-form.

Keep America Beautiful. "KAB: A Beautiful History." KAB.org, www.kab.org/site/PageServer?pagename=kab_history.

Kennedy, John F. "Special Message to the Congress on Urgent National Needs," www.jfklibrary.org/Research/Ready-Reference/JFK-Speeches/Special-Message-to-the-Congress-on-Urgent-National-Needs-May-25-1961.aspx.

Kennedy, John F. "Kennedy Quotations," www.jfklibrary.org/Research/Ready-Reference/JFK-Quotations.aspx.

Kobliner, Beth. *Money as You Grow: 20 Things Kids Need to Know to Live Financially Smart Lives*. Washington, DC: President's Advisory Council on Financial Capability, 2010.

Langer, Ellen J. *Counterclockwise: Mindful Health and the Power of Possibility*. New York: Ballantine Books, 2009.

Logan's Run. Metro-Goldwyn-Mayer movie directed by Michael Anderson. 1976.

Lusardi, Annamaria. "Survey of the States: Economic and Personal Finance Education in our Nation's Schools." Council for Economic Education, www.councilforeconed.org/wp/wp-content/uploads/2011/11/2011-Survey-of-the-States.pdf.

MacLeod, Hugh. "Gaping Void." Blog post, http://us1.campaign-archive2.com/?u=028de8672d5f9a229f15e9edf&id=a61b81c1de&e=6c52ad51d0&socialproxy=http%3A%2F%2Fus1.campaign-archive2.com%2Fsocial-proxy%2Ffacebook-like%3Fu%3D028de8672d5f9a229f15e9edf%26id%3Da61b81c1de.

Marte, Jonnelle, and Linda Lacina. "Living to 100? That Will Be $3.5 M." *SmartMoney*, www.smartmoney.com/retirement/planning/living-to-100-that-will-be-35m-1329867159468.

Mead, Margaret. BrainyQuote.com, www.brainyquote.com/quotes/authors/m/margaret_mead.html.

Mencer, Lisa Kay. "Keep America Beautiful." Learning to Give.org, http://learningto give.org/papers/paper284.html.

Miller, Arthur. *Death of a Salesman*. London: Cresset Press, 1949.

National Center for Health Statistics. *Health, United States, 2011: With Special Feature on Socioeconomic Status and Health*. Washington, DC: National Center for Health Statistics, 2011.

National Foundation for Credit Counseling. "NFCC Polls Reveals Consumers' Top Financial Regrets." www.prweb.com/releases/2012/7/prweb9663024.htm.

National Highway Traffic Safety Administration. "National Seat Belt Enforcement," www.nhtsa.gov/PEAK.

National Retirement Planning Coalition. "Retire on Your Terms," www.retireonyour ownterms.org.

Nelson, Senator Gaylord. Speech delivered on October 8, 1969. *Congressional Record 115*, no. 164 (1969).

Nixon, Richard M. "Peace with Honor." Speech delivered in radio and television broadcast, 1973.

Nyce, Steve. "Retirement Planning in a Post-Crisis Economy." Towers Watson Retirement Attitudes Survey, 2011.

Obama, Barack. "Establishing the President's Council on Financial Capability." The White House Archives, www.whitehouse.gov/sites/default/files/2010 financial.eo_.rel_.pdf.

Passy, Charles. "The Cost of Living Longer—Much Longer." *SmartMoney*, www .smartmoney.com/retirement/planning/the-cost-of-living-longer--much-longer-1328897162395.

Pension Benefit Guaranty Corporation. "Who We Are—Mission Statement." www .pbgc.gov/about/who-we-are.html.

Pension Protection Act. Public Law 109-280, 109th Cong. (2006).

Perez, Sarah. "Google Launches 'Solve for X' Website, The New Home for Its Global Innovations Conference." TechCrunch.com, http://techcrunch.com/2012/02/06/google-launches-solve-for-x-website-the-new-home-for-its-global-innovations-conference.

Perlman, Brian, Kelly Keanneally, and Ilana Boivie. *Pensions and Retirement Security 2011*. National Institute on Retirement Security, 2011.

Pew Research Center. "10,000–Baby Boomers Retire." Pew Research Center, The Databank, 2012, http://pewresearch.org/databank/dailynumber/?NumberID=1150.

Pink, Daniel H. *A Whole New Mind: Why Right-Brainers Will Rule the Future*. New York: Riverhead Trade, 2006.

PlanSponsor Magazine. "Personalities: Rob Portman and Ben Cardin, Republican from Ohio and Democrat from Maryland." *PlanSponsor Magazine*. (2003), www.plansponsor.com/MagazineArticle.aspx?Id=6442455872.

Platt, Brenda and Doug Rowe. *Reduce, Reuse, Refill!* Institute for Local Self-Reliance, http://refillables.grrn.org/ilsr/uploads/assets/pdfs/refill_report.pdf.

Plumer, Bradford. "The Origins of Anti-Litter Campaigns." MotherJones.com, www.motherjones.com/mojo/2006/05/origins-anti-litter-campaigns.

President's Advisory Council on Financial Capability. "National Financial Capability Challenge." U.S. Department of the Treasury, www.challenge.treas.gov/statistics_2011/national_2011.aspx.

Prudential Financial. "Bring Your Challenges." Prudential.com, www.prudential.com/bringyourchallenges/.

RED. Summit Entertainment movie, directed by Robert Schwentke. 2010.

Reed, Jonathan. *The Lost Generation*. http://www.youtube.com/watch?v=42E2fAWM6rA.

Reed, Matthew. *Student Debt and the Class of 2010*. The Institute for College Access and Success, http://projectonstudentdebt.org/files/pub/classof2010.pdf.

Rogers, Heather. *Gone Tomorrow: The Hidden Life of Garbage*. New York: The New Press, 2005.

Roosevelt, Eleanor. "Speech Before the D.C. Branch of the American Association for Social Security, the Council of Social Agencies, and the Monday Evening Club, 1934," www.gwu.edu/~erpapers/documents/articles/oldagepensions.cfm.

Rosenthal, Robert and Lenore Jacobson. *Pygmalion in the Classroom*. New York: Holt, Rinehart & Winston, 1968.

Schultz, P. Welsey, and Steven R. Stein. *Litter in America: National Findings and Recommendations*. Keep America Beautiful, 2009.

Scriven, Michael and Richard Paul. "Defining Critical Thinking." Statement at the 8th Annual International Conference on Critical Thinking and Education Reform, 1987, www.criticalthinking.org/pages/defining-critical-thinking/766.

Sivers, Derek. "Leadership Lessons from Dancing Guy." Speech given at TED Conference, 2010. www.youtube.com/watch?v=V74AxCqOTvg.

Smoking is Ugly. Smokingisugly.com, www.smokingisugly.com/main.html.

Society of Actuaries. Key Findings and Issues: Longevity. 2011 Risks and Process of Retirement Survey Report, 2012.

Stiglitz, Joseph E. "The Book of Jobs." *Vanity Fair*, January 2012.

Strand, Ginger. "The Crying Indian: How an Environmental Icon Helped Sell Cans—and Sell Out Environmentalism." *Orion* (November/December 2008), www.orionmagazine.org/index.php/articles/article/3642.

Taleb, Nassim Nicholas. *The Black Swan: The Impact of the Highly Improbable*. New York: Random House, 2007.

Temporary Assistance for Needy Families. "Welfare Application Instructions." http://tanf-benefits.com.

Tracy, Joe. "Japanese Balloon Bombs." Japanese Balloon Bombs.com, 2008, www.japaneseballoonbombs.com.

Transamerica Center for Retirement Studies. *A Source of Inspiration: Future Early Retirees.* Transamerica Center for Retirement Studies, 12th Annual Transamerica Retirement Survey, 2011.

Transamerica Center for Retirement Studies. *Full-time & Part-time Workers.* Transamerica Center for Retirement Studies, 13th Annual Transamerica Retirement Survey, 2012.

Trollope, Anthony. *The Fixed Period.* Leipzig: Bernhard Tauchnitz, 1882.

The Truth. Argentinian Political Campaign, www.youtube.com/watch?v=ShDoxve85jI.

U.S. Geological Survey. "Fast Facts Study Guide (State Areas)." The US50.com, www.theus50.com/area.php.

U.S. Government Accountability Office. *401(k) Plans: Policy Changes Could Reduce the Long-Term Effects of Leakage on Workers' Retirement Savings.* Report to the Chairman, Special Committee on Aging, U.S. Senate, 2009.

U.S. Office of Personnel Management. *Recruiting, Retaining and Honoring a World-Class Workforce to Serve the American People.* OPM.gov, www.opm.gov/ses/recruitment/ecq.asp.

U.S. Senate Special Committee on Aging. *Saving Smartly for Retirement: Are Americans Being Encouraged to Break Open the Piggy Bank.* Hearing before the Special Committee on Aging, 110th Cong., 2d sess., 2008.

VanDerhei, Jack. *30th Anniversary of the Universal IRA: A Time to Look at All Retirement Savings Today and Going Forward.* Employee Benefit Research Institute, Savings Coalition of America, 2012.

Vanguard Group. "Plan for a Long Retirement." Vanguard Marketing Corporation, https://personal.vanguard.com/us/insights/retirement/plan-for-a-long-retirement-tool.

Vanguard Institutional Investor Group. *How America Saves 2010: A Report on Vanguard 2009 Defined Contribution Plan Data,* https://institutional.vanguard.com/iam/pdf/HAS.pdf.

Watson, Thomas J. BrainyQuote.com, www.brainyquote.com/quotes/quotes/t/thomasjwa130709.html.

Weisman, Mary-Lou. "The History of Retirement, from Early Man to A.A.R.P." *New York Times,* www.nytimes.com/1999/03/21/jobs/the-history-of-retirement-from-early-man-to-aarp.html?pagewanted=all&src=pm.

What Shall We Do With Our Old? Biography Company movie directed by D.W. Griffith. 1911.

Wooten, James A. "The Most Glorious Story of Failure in the Business: The Studebaker Packard Corporation and the Origins of ERISA." *Buffalo Law Review 49* (2001): 683.

Wray, David. "Automatic Enrollment—Not The End, A Great Beginning." Plan Sponsor Council of America, www.psca.org/automatic-enrollment-not-the-end-a-great-beginning.

Wrenn, Mike, and Andy Warhol. *Andy Warhol in His Own Words (In Their Own Words)*. New York: Omnibus Press & Schirmer Trade Books, 1991.

Yeats, William Butler. Quotations Book.com, http://quotationsbook.com/quote/28289.

Glossary

401(k) plan: An employer-sponsored defined contribution plan that enables employees to make tax-deferred contributions from their salaries to the plan. Companies sponsoring these plans often also make contributions, matching the employee's contributions up to a certain percentage.

403(b) plan: An employer-sponsored defined contribution retirement plan that enables employees of universities, public schools, and nonprofit organizations to make tax-deferred contributions from their salaries to the plan.

aggressive: An investment approach that accepts above-average risk of loss in return for potentially above-average investment returns. Contrast to *conservative*.

American Society of Pension Professionals & Actuaries (ASPPA): A nonprofit professional organization of 10,000 plus members which works to educate retirement plan and benefits professionals, while preserving and enhancing the private pension system.

annuity: Form of contract sold by life insurance companies that guarantees a fixed or variable payment to the annuitant at some future time, usually retirement. All capital in the annuity grows tax-deferred.

asset allocation: A method of investing by which investors include a range of different investment classes—such as stocks, bonds, and cash equivalents—in their portfolios. See *diversification*.

assets: Securities, cash, and receivables owned by a person, business, retirement plan, or an investment fund.

automatic escalation: A provision in a defined contribution retirement plan whereby an employer automatically increases the percentage of salary that an employee defers into the retirement plan at a set interval, up to a predetermined maximum percentage. Most often used in plans with automatic enrollment.

automatic enrollment: A provision in a defined contribution retirement plan that allows an employer to automatically enroll employees in the plan at a set deferral rate unless the employee chooses to opt out of the plan or enroll at a different deferral rate.

Baby Boomers: The generation born between 1946 and 1964.

Bear Market: A period during which the majority of securities prices in a particular market (such as the stock market) drop substantially. One generally accepted measure is a price decline of 20 percent or more over at least a two-month period. Contrast to *Bull Market*.

bond: A debt security issued by a company, municipality, or government agency. A bond investor lends money to the issuer and, in exchange, the issuer promises to repay the loan amount on a specified maturity date; the issuer usually pays the bondholder periodic interest payments over the life of the loan.

broker-dealer: A company engaged in the business of buying and selling securities and other financial instruments for others or for their firm.

budget deficit: Excess of spending over income for a government, corporation, or individual over a particular period of time. In reference to the federal government, a budget deficit is also known as the national debt.

Bull Market: A period during which a majority of securities prices in a particular market (such as the stock market) rise substantially. Contrast to *Bear Market*.

collective investment trusts/fund: A fund that is operated by a trust company or a bank and combines the assets of various individuals and organizations to create a larger, well-diversified portfolio.

compounding: The cumulative effect that reinvesting an investment's earnings can have by generating additional earnings of its own. Over time, compounding can produce significant growth in the value of an investment.

conservative: An investment approach that aims to grow capital over the long term, focusing on minimizing risk. Contrast to *aggressive*.

coverage: The proportion of workers who have access to a workplace retirement plan (includes both those who participate in the plan and those who don't).

default: A failure by an issuer to:
1. Pay principal or interest when due.
2. Meet nonpayment obligations, such as reporting requirements.
3. Comply with certain covenants in the document authorizing the issuance of a bond (an indenture).

deferral rate: The proportion of an employee's pretax compensation that is set aside as a contribution to a retirement plan.

defined benefit (DB) plan: An employer-sponsored pension plan where the amount of future benefits an employee will receive from the plan is defined, typically by a formula based on salary history and years of service. Contrast to *defined contribution plan*.

defined contribution (DC) plan: An employer-sponsored retirement plan, such as a 401(k) plan or a 403(b) plan, in which contributions are made to individual participant accounts. Depending on the type of DC plan, contributions may be made by the employee, the employer, or both. The employee's benefits at retirement or termination of employment are based on the employee and employer contributions and earnings and losses on those contributions. See also *401(k) or 403(b) plan*. Contrast to *defined benefit plan*.

diversification: The practice of investing broadly across a number of different securities, industries, or asset classes to reduce risk. Diversification is a key benefit of investing in mutual funds and other investment companies that have diversified portfolios.

Employee Benefit Research Institute (EBRI): A nonprofit organization dedicated to contributing to, encouraging, and enhancing the development of sound employee benefit programs and sound public policy through research and education.

Employee Retirement Income Security Act (ERISA): A 1974 law governing the operation of most private pension and benefit plans, the law eased pension eligibility rules, set up the Pension Benefit Guaranty Corporation, and established guidelines for the management of pension funds.

fiduciary: Person, company, or association holding assets in trust for a beneficiary. The fiduciary is charged with the responsibility of investing the money wisely for the benefit of the beneficiary.

funding risk: The risk that the amount of money a person saves in their retirement plans (together with the appreciation of those assets) won't be enough to fund their retirement.

Generation X: The generation born between 1965 and 1979.

Individual Retirement Account (IRA): A tax-deferred account set up by or for an individual to hold and invest funds for retirement.

inflation: The overall, general upward price movement of goods and services in an economy. Inflation is one of the major risks to investors over the long term because it erodes the purchasing power of savings.

institutional investors: The businesses, nonprofit organizations, corporate retirement plans, and other similar investors who own investment funds and other securities on behalf of their organizations. This classification of investors differs from individual or household investors.

interest/interest rate: The fee charged by a lender to a borrower, usually expressed as an annual percentage of the principal.

Investment Company Institute (ICI): The national association of U.S. investment companies whose mission is to encourage adherence to high ethical standards by all industry participants, advance the interests of funds, and promote public understanding of mutual funds and other investment companies.

investment return: The gain or loss on an investment over a certain period, expressed as a percentage.

investment risk: The possibility of losing some or all of the amounts invested or not gaining value in an investment.

large cap: Stock with a large capitalization (numbers of shares outstanding times the price of the shares). Large-cap stocks typically have at least $5 billion in outstanding market value.

Life Insurance Marketing and Research Association/LIMRA International, Inc. (LIMRA): An association of life insurance and financial services companies with approximately 850 members internationally that conducts research and provides consulting.

longevity risk: The risk of outliving one's life expectancy and using up one's retirement savings and income.

lump sum: Payment of money received at one time instead of in periodic payments. People retiring from or leaving a company may receive a lump-sum distribution of the value of their retirement plan. (Special tax rules apply to such lump-sum distributions unless the money is rolled into an IRA rollover account.)

matching contributions: A type of contribution an employer chooses to make in a defined contribution retirement plan. The contribution is based on the elective deferral contributions made by the employee and often matches that contribution at a set percentage.

mid cap: Stock with a middle-level capitalization (numbers if shares outstanding times the price of the shares). Mid-cap stocks typically have between $1 billion and $5 billion in outstanding market value.

Millennials: The generation born between 1980 and 2000, brought up using digital technology.

mutual fund: A registered investment company that invests in a portfolio of securities selected by a professional investment advisor to meet a specified financial goal (investment objective).

Pension Benefit Guaranty Corporation (PBGC): Federal agency established in 1974 under ERISA that insures defined benefit retirement plans offered by private-sector employers.

pension plan: Retirement plans that provide replacement for salary when a person is no longer working. Employer plans can be defined benefit (DB) or defined contribution (DC) plans.

Pension Protection Act of 2006 (PPA): Congressional pension reform legislation designed to encourage individual retirement savings and to make employer-funded plans subject to stricter regulation.

plan administrator: The person who is identified in the plan document as having responsibility for running the plan. It could be the employer, a committee of employees, a company executive, or someone hired for that purpose.

plan compliance: The oversight of a plan to ensure that it adheres to IRS and Department of Labor rules regarding employee benefits.

plan document: A formal, written document required by the Department of Labor for all retirement plans that detail how a plan operates and its requirements.

plan sponsor: A company or employer that sets up a retirement plan for the benefit of the organization's employees.

portfolio: A collection of securities owned by an individual or an institution that may include stocks, bonds, money market instruments, and other securities.

Qualified Default Investment Alternatives (QDIAs): Default investment for participants who do not choose an investment in a retirement plan. The default accounts include professionally managed accounts, balanced mutual funds, and lifecycle mutual funds.

qualified retirement plan: An employer-sponsored retirement plan that meets the IRS and Employee Retirement Income Security Act of 1974 (ERISA) requirements to have certain tax advantages for employers and employees. Such plans can be defined benefit plans or defined contribution plans.

replacement ratio: The percentage of current income that you would need in retirement to maintain your current standard of living.

retirement ready: The state in which an individual is well-prepared for retirement, should it happen as planned or unexpectedly, and can continue generating adequate income to cover living expenses throughout his/her lifetime through retirement savings and investments, employer pension benefits, government benefits, and/or continuing to work in some manner while allowing for leisure time to enjoy life.

return: The gain or loss of a security in a particular period. It is usually quoted as a percentage.

risk tolerance: An investor's willingness to lose some or all of an investment in exchange for greater potential returns.

Saver's Credit: Tax credit that encourages saving for retirement. Helps people pay less federal tax by contributing to a company-sponsored retirement plan, such as 401(k) plan, or individual retirement account (IRA).

Section 404(c): A section of ERISA that provides voluntary guidelines that a plan sponsor can follow which enable them to effectively transfer the potential liability associated with investment decision-making to employees who participate in a 401(k) or other participant-directed defined contribution plan.

shareholder: An investor who owns shares of a mutual fund or other company.

Silent Generation: The generation born between 1925 and 1945.

small cap: Stocks with a small capitalization (numbers of shares outstanding times the price of the shares). Small-cap stocks typically have less than $1 billion in outstanding market value.

stable value fund: An investment fund that seeks to preserve principal and to provide consistent returns and liquidity. Stable value funds include collective investment funds sponsored by banks or trust companies or contracts issued by insurance companies.

stock: A share of ownership or equity in a corporation.

target date fund: A fund that invests in a mix of asset classes and follows a predetermined reallocation of risk over time for a person expecting to retire at the target date of the fund. They typically rebalance portfolios over time to become more conservative and income producing.

Third-Party Administrator (TPA): An entity other than a plan sponsor that is responsible for administering a workplace retirement plan.

Treasury Inflation Protected Securities (TIPS): U.S. Treasury securities issued at a fixed rate of interest but with principal adjusted every six months based on changes in the Consumer Price Index. TIPS sacrifice some yield as a tradeoff for the inflation protection.

vesting: Right an employee gradually acquires by length of service at a company to receive employer-contributed benefits, such as matching contributions to the retirement plan. By law, employees must be vested 100 percent after a maximum of seven years.

List of Contributors

Nevin Adams

Nevin Adams joined the Employee Benefit Research Institute (EBRI) as Director, Education and External Relations and Co-Director, EBRI Center for Research on Retirement Income (CRI) in 2011, and was named Director of the American Savings Education Council (ASEC) in May 2012. EBRI is a nonprofit, nonpartisan research and education firm located in Washington, DC. Prior to that he spent a dozen years as Global Editor-in-Chief of *PLANSPONSOR* magazine and its web counterpart, plansponsor.com, as well as *PLANADVISER* and *PLANSPONSOR* Europe magazines, and was the creator, writer, and publisher of plansponsor.com's *NewsDash*, the industry's leading daily source for information focused on the critical issues impacting benefits industry professionals. Before that he spent two decades in senior management positions at two large national financial institutions working with workplace retirement plans. He graduated summa cum laude with a BS in finance from DePaul University in Chicago, Illinois, and in 1988 he received his JD, also from DePaul University.

Ted Benna

Ted Benna is commonly referred to as "the father of 401(k)" because he created and gained IRS approval of the first 401(k) savings plan. He has received many citations for his accomplishments, including the 2001 National Jefferson Award for Greatest Public Service by a Private Citizen and the 2001 Player of the Year Award, selected by *Defined Contribution News*. He was one of eight individuals selected by *Money* magazine for its special 20th Anniversary Hall of Fame issue, was selected by *Business Insurance* as one of the four People of the Century,

167

was one of 10 selected by *Mutual Fund Market News* for its special 10th Anniversary Legends in Our Own Time issue, and received the Lifetime Achievement Award by *Defined Contribution News* in 2005. Ted has authored four books, the latest of which is 401(k)s *For Dummies*.

Kent G. Callahan

Kent Callahan is a member of the Transamerica U.S. Management Board and serves as President and CEO of the Employer Solutions & Pension (ES&P) division, which serves more than 34,000 institutional customers and 3.2 million American workers.

Kent has dedicated more than 30 years to the financial services industry, including 25 years with AEGON/Transamerica. He is a frequent speaker at major pension industry events throughout the United States and globally. Kent has been named by 401kWire.com as one of the top 50 "Most Influential People in Defined Contribution. Kent also serves as a member of LIMRA's Pension Leadership Committee and is Chairman of the Transamerica Center for Retirement Studies.

John Carl

John Carl is Founder and President of Retirement Learning Center, the nation's preeminent thought leader on retirement issues, as well as founding lecturer for The Retirement Advisor University (TRAU) at UCLA Anderson School of Management Executive Education, and Executive Director of the *PLANSPONSOR* Institute, the education and training arm of *PLANSPONSOR*. John released his first book in 2009, *Retirement Resource Guide: Essential ERISA Education & Best Practices for Financial Advisors,* which received an APEX Grand Award for publishing excellence. For 2012, 401kWire.com identified John as one of the most influential individuals in the 401(k) industry for the sixth consecutive year.

Catherine Collinson

Catherine Collinson serves as President of the Transamerica Center for Retirement Studies, and is a retirement and market trends expert and champion for Americans who are at risk of not achieving a financially secure retirement. Catherine oversees all research and outreach initiatives, including the Annual Transamerica Retirement Survey.

With over 15 years of retirement services experience, Catherine has become a nationally recognized voice on retirement trends for the industry. She has testified before Congress on matters related to employer-sponsored retirement plans among small businesses, which have featured the need to raise awareness of the Saver's Credit among those who would benefit most from the important tax credit. Catherine is regularly cited by top media outlets on retirement-related topics. Her expert commentary has appeared in major publications, including: the *Wall Street Journal, U.S. News & World Report, USA Today, Money,* the *New York Times, Huffington Post, Kiplinger's, CBS MoneyWatch, Los Angeles Times, Chicago Tribune, Employee Benefits News,* and *HR Magazine.* She has also appeared on PBS' *Nightly Business Report,* NPR's *Marketplace,* and CBS affiliates throughout the country.

Catherine earned her BA in British and American literature at Scripps College, Claremont, California, and her MBA at the University of California, Irvine.

Paul D'Aiutolo

Paul D'Aiutolo is an Institutional Consultant at UBS Financial Services. Primarily focused on providing fiduciary and risk management services to corporate investment committees, and educational services to the participants they govern, Paul leads a team with over 100 institutional clients with assets in excess of $1 billion. Paul has been acknowledged by numerous industry associations as an influential voice and advocate, including 2012 recognition as a Top Ten Mid-Market Advisor by 401kWire.com and a finalist for the 2009 *PLANSPONSOR* and *PLANADVISER* Retirement Plan Advisor of the Year.

Mike DiCenso

Mike DiCenso is the National Practice Leader at Gallagher Retirement Services and the President of Gallagher Fiduciary Advisors, LLC. Mike has more than 25 years of experience in the retirement plan arena and is considered a thought leader on issues such as fiduciary process management, fee transparency, and industry trends. In 2008, 2009, and

2010 Mike was recognized as one of the most influential people in the 401(k) industry by 401kWire.com and was accepted into the Retirement Advisory Council in 2011.

Brian H. Graff

Brian Graff began serving as the Executive Director/Chief Executive Officer of ASPPA in 1996. Brian actively speaks on behalf of the employer-sponsored pension system and has been quoted in the *Washington Post* and the *Wall Street Journal*, as well as interviewed on Bloomberg TV. In 2011, he testified before the U.S. Department of Labor on the proposed definition of fiduciary regulation, and was instrumental in the creation of the National Association of Plan Advisers (NAPA)—the first organization dedicated to serving retirement plan advisors.

Brian received his doctoral degree in law, cum laude, from the University of Pennsylvania Law School in Philadelphia. He holds a BS in accounting with distinction from Cornell University in Ithaca, NY.

Paul S. Henry

Paul Henry is the Managing Director of Retirement Clients and Products at LIMRA International. Paul has more than 25 years of experience in the financial services industry, including 20 years as a strategist, head of marketing, and head of product development for industry leaders in the retirement market. In his current role, Paul is responsible for ensuring that LIMRA members who are, or seek to be, active in the retirement market fully benefit from LIMRA's wide range of industry-leading resources, including research, compliance support, training, and consulting services.

J. Mark Iwry

Mark Iwry is Senior Advisor to the Secretary of the Treasury and is the Deputy Assistant Secretary for Retirement and Health Policy at the U.S. Treasury Department. Mark was previously a Nonresident Senior Fellow at the Brookings Institution, Research Professor at Georgetown University, Of Counsel to the law firm of Sullivan & Cromwell LLP, and a Principal of the Retirement Security Project. He was the Treasury

Department's Benefits Tax Counsel (1995–2001), serving as the principal official directly responsible for tax policy and regulation relating to the nation's qualified pension and 401(k) plans, employer health plans, and other employee benefits, and previously was a partner in the law firm of Covington & Burling LLP. Mark has often testified before congressional committees—representing the Treasury and Executive Branch or, while in the private sector, testifying as an independent expert—and State legislatures; has advised numerous Senators, members of Congress, and their staffs on both sides of the aisle, as well as various Presidential campaigns. In recent years, Mark has been recognized as one of the 30 Top Financial Players (*Smart Money* magazine), one of the 100 Most Influential People in Finance and one of five in the field of Retirement and Benefits (*Treasury and Risk* magazine), one of the 100 Most Influential People in the 401(k) Industry (401kWire.com), *InvestmentNews* Power 20 (20 individuals expected to have a major influence on the financial services industry).

Todd Lacey

Todd Lacey is the Senior Vice President of Strategic Distribution at Transamerica Retirement Solutions. Prior to joining Transamerica, Todd was President and Founder of The (k)Larity Group, a retirement plan consulting firm. Lacey is a frequent speaker at national conferences and is actively involved in multiple organizations, including as co-chair of the ASPPA 401(k) Summit. He also serves as a Board of Director member for the ASPPA Benefits Council of Atlanta and the ASPPA Investment Professional Committee. He is co-editor of the ASPPA *Advisor Update*, a bimonthly newsletter delivered to thousands of advisors across the country.

Chad J. Larsen

Chad Larsen is the President of Moreton Retirement Partners. Chad has worked with hundreds of employers helping them to implement prudent processes that have improved the participant outcomes of their plans. He is a frequent national speaker for the retirement industry and has given numerous retirement plan workshops to educate employers on the key elements of successful retirement plans.

Chad was recently inducted into the 2011 Advisor Hall of Fame by *PLANADVISER* magazine, and was also selected as the 2007 Retirement Plan Advisor of the year by *PLANSPONSOR* magazine.

Joseph J. Masterson

Joseph J. Masterson, Senior Vice President and Chief Marketing Officer of Transamerica Retirement Solutions, was a founder of DIVERSIFIED and is a member of their Senior Leadership Team.

Joe is past Chairperson of the Retirement & Investment Marketing Committee – LIMRA International; a longstanding member of AIMSE; a member of the Investment Management Consultants Association; a member of the editorial advisory board of the *Journal of Pension Benefits*; a member of the Legg Mason Retirement Advisory Council; EACH Enterprise From Research to Sales Success Advisory Board, and DCIIA founding board. He is a frequent speaker and author on retirement plans and asset allocation strategies.

He has helped many organizations address their pension concerns and arrive at client-driven solutions. He is a leader in helping people save and invest wisely for retirement, coining the phrase "Save 10." He was named 19th "Most Influential Person in the 401(k) Industry" in 2012 by 401kWire.com.

J. Fielding Miller

J. Fielding Miller is the CEO of CAPTRUST Financial Advisors. As an early pioneer in the retirement advice industry, Fielding is a frequent speaker and active participant in various industry associations and recognized as one of the 2012 Top 50 "Most Influential People in Defined Contribution." He is also the recipient of the first ever *PLANADVISER* Magazine Lifetime Achievement Award in 2012.

John B. Mott

With more than 30 years in the financial services industry, John B. Mott focuses on the management and design of qualified and nonqualified retirement plans and is responsible for over 50 corporate plans across the country that make up over 100,000 plan participants. John also holds the **PLANSPONSOR** Retirement Professional (**PRP**) designation.

He won the 2005 Retirement Plan Advisor of the Year by *PLANSPON-SOR* magazine. He was also recognized as one of the nation's 2010 Top 100 Adviser and Adviser Teams by *PLANADVISER* magazine.

Joseph W. Mrozek

As Managing Director and Head of Small and Middle Markets Sales for Global Wealth and Retirement Services (GWRS) and the Business and Global Commercial Banks, Joe Mrozek is responsible for sales in the $0–$100 million market segment for the Institutional Retirement and Benefits Services (IRBS) Group at Bank of America Merrill Lynch. At Bank of America Merrill Lynch, "We help people at work attain financially secure futures in a world where it is increasingly hard to do so."

Fred Reish

Fred Reish is the Partner/Chair, Fiduciary Services ERISA Team at Drinker Biddle & Reath, LLP. He has been recognized as one of the Legends of the retirement industry by both *PLANADVISER* magazine and *PLANSPONSOR* magazine. Fred also received awards for: the 401(k) Industry's Most Influential Person by 401kWire.com; the Commissioner's Award and District Director's Award by the IRS; the Edison Founder's Award by the American Society of Professionals and Actuaries (ASPPA); the Institutional Investor and the *PLANSPONSOR* magazine Lifetime Achievement Awards; and the ASPPA/Morningstar 401(k) Leadership Award. He co-chaired the IRS Los Angeles Benefits Conference for over 10 years, served as a founding co-chair of the ASPPA 401(k) Summit, and has served on the Steering Committee for the DOL National Conference.

Charles Ruffel

Charles Ruffel is the Managing Partner at Kudu Advisors. Charles is a leading authority on global pension issues, institutional money management, and international securities services. Prior to founding Kudu Advisors, Charles was the Founder and CEO of Asset International and was a financial journalist with *Institutional Investor*, New York, and *Financial Mail*, Johannesburg.

Dallas Salisbury

Dallas Salisbury, President and CEO of the Employee Benefit Research Institute (EBRI), joined EBRI at its founding in Washington, DC, in 1978. As a member of a number of commissions, Mr. Salisbury assists study panels as well as editorial advisory boards. He is a Fellow of the National Academy of Human Resources. He currently serves as an appointee of President Obama on the PBGC Advisory Committee (having served in the late 1980s as an appointee of President H. W. Bush) and an appointee of the Comptroller General of the United States to his Board of Advisors. He is a past member of the Board of the NAHR, the NAHR Foundation, the Securities and Exchange Commission Investor Advisory Committee, the Board of Directors for FINRA Investor Education Foundation, on the Secretary of Labor's ERISA Advisory Council, Board of Directors of the Society for Human Resources Management, U.S. Advisory Panel on Medicare Education, and the Board of Directors of the National Academy of Social Insurance.

Dallas has been honored with the *Award for Professional Excellence* from the Society for Human Resource Management, the *PLANSPONSOR* Lifetime Achievement Award, and the Keystone Award of *WorldatWork*, and in 2012 the Public Service Award of the International Foundation of Employee Benefit Plans. Dallas was a delegate to the 1998, 2002, and 2006 National Summits on Retirement Savings, and the 2005 White House Conference on Aging. Dallas accepted a 2007 National Emmy Award for *Savingsman* and the *Choose to Save*® public education program.

Jay Vivian

Jay Vivian retired in late 2007 as head of IBM's $135 billion retirement funds system, where he led the funds' successful weathering of 2001 to 2002's financial perfect storm, several benefit redesigns, and oversaw implementation of asset diversification and LDI. He is on the board of ICMA-RC, the investment/pension committee of United Way Worldwide, and is on the Committee on Investment of Employee Benefit Assets (CIEBA). *PLANSPONSOR* magazine named IBM Plan Sponsor of the Year in 2006, *Treasury & Risk* named him one of the 100 Most Influential People in Finance in 2007, and *PLANSPONSOR* gave him their Lifetime Achievement Award in 2010. He has been featured in articles and interviews in the *Wall Street Journal*, *USA Today*, *MSN Money*, *P&I*, *Institutional Investor*, and *aiCIO*.

Index

A

AARP U@50 contest, 66–67

Adams, Nevin, 48–50, 60, 108, 110, 115

Ad Council, 76, 77, 78

Advertising campaigns, 72

Advisors. *See* Retirement plan advisors

Aggressive, definition of, 161

American Express Company, 20

American Recovery and Reinvestment Act, 115

Americans, all, letter to, 143–145

American Social Security system, 25

American Society of Pension Professionals & Actuaries (ASPPA), 161

Annuity, 54, 161

Annuity Puzzle, 100

APFs. *See* Automatic Plan Features (APFs)

Apollo 13 (movie), 31–33

Apple Inc., 127

ASPPA. *See* American Society of Pension Professionals & Actuaries (ASPPA)

Asset allocation, 161

Assets, 161

Audia, Pino, 127

Automatic enrollment, 93–94, 95, 113, 161

Automatic escalation, 93, 95–98, 161

Automatic Plan Features (APFs), 92–93

B

Baby Boomers, 2, 5, 10–11, 28, 49, 161

Bach, David, 14

Bacon, Sir Francis, 43

Bandura, Albert, 106

Bankruptcy, retirees and, 45

BBC. *See* British Broadcasting Corporation (BBC)

Bear market, 161

Behaviors, new, fostering, 137–138

Beliefs, power of, 82–83

Benartzi, Shlomo, 55, 89–90, 92, 136

Benefit plans, 1, 15

Benna, Ted, 49, 51, 64

The Birth of a Nation (movie), 19

Bismarck, Otto von, 23–24

The Black Swan (Taleb), 43

Bloom's Taxonomy, 61

Bond, definition of, 162

British Broadcasting Corporation (BBC), 85

Broker-dealer, 162

Budget deficit, 63, 162

Bull market, definition of, 162

Bureau of Labor Statistics, 6

Burson-Marsteller's 2011 Crisis Preparedness study, 1

Bush, George W., 62
Business world, 126–127

C
Callahan, Kent, 62
Cardin, Ben, 116
Carl, John, 50
Carstensen, Laura L., 6
Centenarian, American, 6
Centers for Disease Control and
    Prevention (CDC), 79
CES. *See* Committee on Economic
    Security (CES)
Chambers, John, 128
Civilized society, hallmark of,
    34–35
Click It Or Ticket, 74, 78–79
Clinton Global Initiative, 16
Cody, Iron Eyes, 129
Coffman, Julia, 74
Collective investment trusts/funds,
    162
Collinson, Catherine, 94
Committee on Economic Security
    (CES), 24, 25
Company-sponsored retirement
    plans, 37
Compounding, definition of, 162
Conservative, definition of, 162
Consumerism, 108
Context, power of, 85–101
Corporate pension plans, 20
Corporate retirement plans, 37
Costa, Dora L., 21, 24, 25, 26
*The Cost of Living Longer—Much
    Longer* (Passy), 6
*Counterclockwise: Mindful Health
    and the Power of Possibility*
    (Langer), 85, 104
Coverage, 91–92, 136, 162

D
D'Aiutolo, Paul, 5, 61, 113–114, 146
The Dancing Man, 142, 150
DB plans. *See* Defined benefit (DB)
    plans
DC plans. *See* Defined contribution
    (DC) plans
Death of a Salesman (Miller), 21
Default, definition of, 162
Deferral rate, definition of, 162
Defined benefit (DB) plans, 1
    challenges of, 52
    definition of, 162
    early days of, 23
    factors leading to underfunding,
        45–47
    as liability to companies, 43–44
    underfunded, 44–45
    vs. defined contribution plans, 15,
        52, 98
Defined contribution (DC) plans:
    definition of, 162
    lower and middle-income
        earners, 7
    organizations, 44
    rise of, 50–52
    success of, 2
    vs. defined benefit plans, 15, 52, 98
Department of Labor (DOL), 39
DiCenso, Mike, 2, 3, 56
Diversification, definition of, 162
DOL. *See* Department of Labor
    (DOL)
Duhigg, Charles, 9
du Pont, Thomas Coleman, 22

E
EBRI. *See* Employee Benefit
    Research Institute, 2, 47, 97, 163
Echo Boomers. *See* Millennials

Economic Growth and Tax Relief
Reconciliation Act of 2001
(EGTRRA), 50, 116
Economic Stimulus Act of 2008,
115
EGTRRA. *See* Economic Growth and
Tax Relief Reconciliation Act of
2001 (EGTRRA)
80% income replacement ratio, 33
Eli Lilly's InnoCentive, 16
Employee Benefit Research Institute
(EBRI). *See* EBRI
Employee Retirement Income
Security Act (ERISA), 36, 39,
44–45, 55, 163
Employees, investment choices of,
52
Employer retirement plans, 39
Employer-sponsored retirement
plan, participation in, 136
ERISA. *See* Employee Retirement
Income Security Act (ERISA)
*The Evolution of Retirement: An
American Economic History
1880–1990* (Costa), 21
Executive Office of the President—
Council of Economic Advisers
report, 99–100

F
Federal Reserve report (July, 2011),
107
"Feed the Pig" (initiative), 61
*Fidelity Thought Leadership: Auto-
Enrollment,* 95
Fiduciary, 163
Figliuolo, Mike, 129
Financial dignity, 34, 35
Financial literacy:
defining, 60–64

improving, 64–69
state of, arguments about, 14
Financial regrets, 143–145
Financial security, in retirement,
34–35
Financial services industry, 73–74,
82, 140, 141
*First Follwer: Leadership Lessons
from the Dancing Guy* (video),
142
The Fixed Period (Trollope), 21
Forbes, 73
Ford, Gerald, 44
401(k) account, average balance of
Americans in, 1
401(k) plan, 1, 36
annuity in, 54
definition of, 161
evolution of, 54–56
portability of, 51, 52
*401(k) Plans: A 25-Year
Retrospective* (Investment
Company Institute), 50
401(k) Savings Act of 2011, 98
401(k) Whisperers, 41, 63, 113, 114,
116, 152
403(b) plan, 36, 161
Frost, Mathew, 57–59, 63, 64–65, 68
Funding risk, 163
Future Early Retirees, 4, 8, 11–13

G
Gaping Void blog post, 130
"Garage" phenomenon (Audia),
127
Generation X, 28, 163
Generation Y, 2
Giant Robot (magazine), 127
Gladwell, Malcolm, 72
Glossary, 161–166

Gone Tomorrow: The Hidden Life of Garbage (Rogers), 78

Google, 127

Google's Solve for X, 16

Goss, Stephen C., 7

Government resolve, 114–117

Graebner, William, 22, 23, 26

Graff, Brian, 51, 54

Greenspan, Alan, 60

Greenwald, Bruce, 107

Griffith, D. W., 19

H

Haley, Amy, 8–9, 12, 13, 16, 109, 145

Hargadon, Andrew, 140

Harvard Business Review (magazine), 123

Heath, Chip, 122, 125

Heath, Dan, 122, 125

Henry, Paul, 33, 112, 115

Hewlett, Bill, 128

Hewlett-Packard, 127, 128

Highway Beautification Act of 1965, 82

History of 401(k) Plans (EBRI's report), 51

History of Retirement: The Meaning and Function of an American Institution (Graebner), 22

Hopkins, Claude C., 9–10

Horvath, David, 127

How Breakthroughs Happen: The Surprising Truth About How Companies Innovate (Hargadon), 140

I

ICI. *See* Investment Company Institute (ICI)

Individual resolve, 106–109

Individual retirement account (IRA), 2

Individuals, retirement readiness and, 1–2

Industry resolve, 112–114

Inflation, definition of, 163

Innovation, disruptive, 73

Institute for Local Self-Reliance, 77

Institutional investor, definition of, 163

Institutional Investor (magazine), 93

Interest/interest rate, definition of, 163

Internal Revenue Code, 36

Internal Revenue Service (IRS), 39, 51

Investment choices, employees and, 52

Investment Company Institute (ICI), 1–2, 50, 163

Investment returns:
  defined benefit plans and, 46–47
  definition of, 163

Investment risk, 163

IRA. *See* Individual Retirement Account, 2

IRS. *See* Internal Revenue Service (IRS)

Iwry, Mark, 91, 95–96, 116, 136

J

Jain, Naveen, 73

James, William, 9

Johnson, Lady Bird, 78, 82

K

KAB. *See* Keep America Beautiful (KAB) campaign, 73, 77–82, 87–88, 100

Kendall, Kenneth, 86

Kennedy, John F., 3, 32, 139
Kim, Sun-Min, 127

L
Lacey, Todd, 14, 16
The Lady with the Lamp, 125
Langer, Ellen, 85–86, 104, 137
Large cap, definition of, 163
Larsen, Chad, 64, 109, 119
Latte Factor®, 13
Leakage, 98–99, 137
Legg Mason Advisory Council, 116
Life expectancy, 2, 6, 15
LIMRA. *See* Life Insurance Marketing
    and Research Association/
    LIMRA International, Inc.
    (LIMRA), 163
Littering, context of, 87–90
Logan's Run (movie), 5
Loman, Willy, 21
Longevity, 47, 52–54, 99–101, 137
Longevity risk, 15, 54, 99, 164
Lower-income households, saving
    for retirement of, 7
Low-income earners, participation
    in contribution plan, 7
Lump sum, definition of, 164
Lusardi, Annamaria, 60

M
*Made to Stick: Why Some Ideas
    Survive and Others Die* (Heath
    and Heath), 122, 125
Marketing the senior citizen,
    26–27
Matching contributions, 11, 164
McDonald's Corporation, 93
McKee, Robert, 123
McLeod, Hugh, 130
Medical profession, Nightingale,
    123–126

Mid cap, definition of, 164
Middle-income earners,
    participation in contribution
    plan, 7
Millennials, 2, 28, 49, 164
Miller, Arthur, 21
Miller, Fielding, 72, 118
*Money As You Grow: 20 Things Kids
    Need To Know To Live
    Financially Smart Lives*
    (website), 62, 63, 144
Morgan, Joy Elmer, 27
Morgenthau, Henry, 25
Mott, John, 55–56, 103–104,
    105, 111
Mrozek, Joe, 3, 59
Mutual fund, definition of, 164

N
Nakamura, Eric, 127
National Aeronautics and Space
    Administration (NASA), 32
National Council for Excellence in
    Critical Thinking, 60
National Forest Service, 82
National Foundation for Credit
    Counseling (NFCC), 143
National Highway Traffic Safety
    Administration (NHTSA), 79
National Industrial Conference
    Board, 27
National Institute on Retirement
    Security (NIRS), 4, 5
National social insurance system,
    23–24
National Women's Health Network
    claims, 79
Net generation. *See* Millennials
New York Times, 20
NFCC. *See* National Foundation for
    Credit Counseling (NFCC)

NHTSA. *See* National Highway Traffic Safety Administration (NHTSA)

Nightingale, Florence, 123–126, 128

90–10–90 plan success metrics, 90, 92–95, 100, 136

NIRS. *See* National Institute on Retirement Security (NIRS)

Nonagenarians, 6–7

Notes on Hospitals (Nightingale), 124

Notes on Nursing (Nightingale), 124

O

Obama, Barack, 62

Office of War Information, 76

"Old Age Pensions" (Roosevelt), 26

One Piece of Paper: The Simple Approach to Powerful, Personal Leadership (Figliuolo), 129

Organizations, retirement readiness, 1

The Origins of Anti-Litter Campaigns (Plumer), 78

Osler, William, 21

Outliers: The Story of Success (Gladwell), 72

Overspending, habitual, 143–145

P

Passy, Charles, 6, 7

PBGC. *See* Pension Benefit Guaranty Corporation (PBGC)

Pension, politics, 23–26

Pension Benefit Guaranty Corporation (PBGC), 45, 164

Pension plan(s), 1, 20, 22–23, 164

Pension Protection Act (PPA) of 2006, 50, 92, 116, 164

Pensions and Retirement Security 2011: A Roadmap for Policymakers (National Institute on Retirement Security), 4

Perkins, George W., 22

Personal finance, 57–59

Pink, Daniel, 3

Plan administrator, 164

Plan compliance, 164

Plan document, 164

Plan performance metrics, 136–137

Plan providers. *See* Recordkeepers/ plan providers

Plan sponsor, 38, 164

Plan Sponsor Council of America (PSCA), 94

Plan Sponsor/Employer, letter to, 145–147

PLANSPONSOR (magazine), 148

Plan sponsor resolve, 109–112

Policymakers, letter to, 147–150

Politics, pension, 23–26

Portman, Rob, 116

The Power of Habit: Why We Do What We Do in Life and Business (Duhigg), 9

PPA. *See* Pension Protection Act (PPA) of 2006

President's Advisory Council on Financial Capability, 62

President's Advisory Council on Financial Literacy, 62

Private defined benefit plans, 22

Private pension plans, 22

Profit Sharing Council of America (PSCA), 94

PSA. *See* Public Service Announcement (PSA)

PSCA. *See* Plan Sponsor Council of America (PSCA); Profit Sharing Council of America (PSCA)
Public Communication Campaign Evaluation: An Environmental Scan of Challenges, Criticisms, Practice, and Opportunities (Coffman), 74
Public Service Announcement (PSA), 78
Public-will campaigns, 74

Q
Qualified default investment alternatives (QDIAs), 39, 93, 97, 164
Qualified retirement plan industry, 35–36, 39
Qualified retirement plans, 36, 38–39, 165

R
Railroad Retirement System, 24
"Ready to Retire" application, 33
Recession, Future Early Retirees and, 12
Recombinant Innovation, 140
Recordkeepers/plan providers, 37
RED (Retired Extremely Dangerous) (movie), 19
Reed, Jonathan, 66–67
Regulations, retirement plans, 39
Reish, Fred, 14, 15, 40
Replacement ratio, 5, 33, 165
Resolve:
    government, 114–117
    individual, 106–109
    industry, 112–114
    plan sponsor, 109–112

stakeholder, 105–106
upping, 139–142
Responsibility, personal, retirement readiness and, 2–4
Retirees, company bankruptcy and, 45
Retirement. *See also* Retirement industry success metrics; Retirement plans; Retirement readiness
    comfortable, 4–7
    in early part of twentieth century, 20
    lower-income households and saving for, 7
    marketing the senior citizen, 26–27
    not saving enough for, 143–145
    politics and pension, 23–26
    rise of, 20–23
    self-efficacy beliefs around, 108–109
    vision of, 28–29
Retirement in an Era of Long Life (Carstensen), 6
Retirement income deficit, 134
Retirement industry success metrics:
    coverage, 91–92
    leakage, 98–99
    longevity, 99–101
    90-10-90 plan, 90, 92–95, 100
Retirement plan advisors, 38–41
Retirement plan industry, 138
Retirement plan lawyers, 38–41
Retirement Planning News (magazine), 27
Retirement plans:
    corporate, 37
    coverage, 91–92
    investments and, 37
    employer, 39, 136
    survey on, 111

Retirement readiness:
  at an individual level, 1–2
  definition of, 165
  financial literacy, 60
  introduction of Super Savers, 7–17
  lesson for, 129–130
  letters to the stakeholders,
    143–152
  littering issue *vs.*, 88–89
  meaning of, 5–7
  at the organizational level, 1
  personal responsibility in, 2–4
  tackling, 73–74
Retirement savings, belief in,
  103–105
Retirement services industry, 41, 89,
  93, 150–152
Retire on Your Terms (National
  Retirement Planning Coalition),
  61
Return, definition of, 165
Revenue Act of 1978, 50
Risk tolerance, definition of, 165
Rockwell, Norman, 76
Rogers, Heather, 78
Role models, campaign, 74–77
Roosevelt, Eleanor, 26
Roosevelt, Franklin Delano, 24
Rosie the Riveter, 74, 75–76
Ruffell, Charlie, 113, 151

S
Salesmanship (magazine), 22
Salisbury, Dallas, 49
Saturday Evening Post, 76
*Save More Tomorrow: Practical
  Behavioral Finance Solutions to
  Improve 401(k) Plans*
  (Benartzi), 55, 89–90, 92, 136
Saver's Credit, 50, 165

SavingAmerica website, 142
Savings:
  for Boomers, 2
  inadequately, 143–145
  learning about, 64–69
  workplace, 135–138
SEAL 401(k) Savings Act, 98, 137
Section 404(c), 165
Self-efficacy, 105–106
"Self-Efficacy: Toward a Unifying
  Theory of Behavior Change"
  (Bandura), 106
Senior Citizen, 27
Senior citizen, marketing, 26–27
Seuss Geisel, Theodor, 29
Shareholder, definition of, 165
Silent Generation, 49, 165
Sivers, Derek, 142
Small cap, definition of, 165
Smokey Bear, 74, 76–77
Smoking is Ugly Campaign, 79–82
Social media, 141
Social Security, 1, 7
Social Security Act, 25
Social Security Old Age Insurance,
  24–25
*A Source of Inspiration: Future Early
  Retirees* (TCRS report), 8, 11
Stable value fund, 165
Stakeholder resolve, 105–106
Stiglitz, Joseph E., 107
Stock, definition of, 165
"Storytelling That Moves People: A
  Conversation with
  Screenwriting Coach Robert
  McKee" (McKee), 123
Straw Man campaign, 130–131
Studebaker Corporation, 44–45
Success, personalizing, 33–34
Super Savers, 4, 7–17

Survey of the States: Economic and Personal Finance: Education in Our Nation's Schools 2011 (Council for Economic Education report), 63

T
Taleb, Nassim Nicholas, 43
Target date fund, definition of, 165
TCRS. *See* Transamerica Center for Retirement Studies (TCRS)
10 percent lifetime savings rate, 135–136
"The History of Retirement, from Early Man to A.A.R.P." (Weisman), 20
Third-party administrator (TPA), 36, 38, 165
Thirteenth Annual Transamerica Center for Retirement Studies survey, 111
TIPS. *See* Treasury Inflation Protected Securities (TIPS)
The Times of London, 124, 125
Towers Watson, 10, 13
TPA. *See* Third-party administrator (TPA)
Traditional pension plans, 1
Transamerica Center for Retirement Studies (TCRS), 4, 8, 11
Treasury Inflation Protected Securities (TIPS), 165–166
Trollope, Anthony, 21
The Truth (anti-smoking campaign), 74–75
Turlington, Christy, 79–80
Turlington Christy's Smoking, 75
Twelfth Annual Transamerica Retirement Survey, 8, 11, 12

Twentieth century:
concept of retirement in, 28
pension plan in, 23
pension provisions, 20
2011 Retirement Attitudes survey, 10

U
Uglydoll (love story), 127–128
Underfunding:
DB plans, factors leading to, 45–47
defined benefit plans and, 44–45
Union Army veterans, retirement of, 20
U.S. National Highway Safety Bureau, 80

V
Values, communicating, 128–129
Vanity Fair, 107
Vesting, 166
Victoria (movie), 19
Vision, retirement and, 28–29
Vivian, Jay, 17, 53, 112

W
Warhol, Andy, 143
War Manpower Commission, 76
War on Terror, 3
Watson, Thomas J., 152
Weisman, Mary-Lou, 20
What Shall We Do With Our Old? (movie), 19–20
A Whole New Mind: Why Right-Brainers Will Rule the Future (Pink), 3
Why Baby Boomers Will Need to Work Longer (McKinsey & Co. Report), 11
Withdrawal rate, 3

Workplace savings, vision for, 135–138
World Health Organization, 79
World Innovation Institute, 73
Wray, David, 94
(Wall Street Journal) Article: "The Rest of the Story", 95

Y

Yeats, W. B., 26
Yes, and technique, 136, 140
The Young Ones (documentary), 85–87, 89, 100, 118, 137, 138

About the Authors

Stig Nybo

Stig Nybo believes that every American worker should be able to retire with confidence. Named by 401kWire.com as one of the top 20 most influential individuals in the retirement industry, Stig has authored articles in retirement industry trade publications and the national press. As a frequent contributor to industry thought leadership, he also offers commentary as an industry expert, speaker, and panelist at major financial services conferences and events and is often quoted in the national press in publications from *PLANSPONSOR* magazine to the *Wall Street Journal*.

Stig currently serves as President of Pension Sales and Distribution for Transamerica Retirement Solutions, a leading U.S. retirement plan provider. He has a passion for the retirement plan industry and has committed more than 20 years to promoting best practices for qualified retirement plans. He serves on the board of the Transamerica Center for Retirement Studies, a nonprofit corporation and private operating foundation that studies retirement trends and issues facing the American workforce. His leadership has resulted in innovation that retirement plan sponsors and their financial advisors use to help plan participants save and invest wisely for their retirement.

Stig currently lives in Portola Valley, California with his wife, Holly, and two boys, Andreas and Torsten.

Liz Alexander, PhD

Liz Alexander's gift and passion is helping individuals and organizations transition from experts to thought leaders. She is an author, business book strategist, and consulting co-author who has for the past 25 years worked on both sides of the Atlantic. Liz also collaborates with aspiring business authors and thought leaders in India.

She has written 11 nonfiction books and co-authored three others. In addition to consulting and speaking around the world, Liz developed and teaches the Strategic Communication Certificate Program for the Professional Development Center at The University of Texas at Austin, where she earned her PhD in Educational Psychology.

Liz lives in Austin, Texas with her beloved black Labrador, Buffy.